GOWER COAST SHIPWRECKS

CARL SMITH

Sou'wester Books

ISBN 0 9515281 4 9

Published by Sou'wester Books,
1 Bryn Tirion, Clydach, Swansea. SA6 5LB

Printed by Walters Printers, Clydach, Swansea.

CONTENTS

Introduction 5

Sugar, Salt and Elephant's Teeth 11

Coal and Copper Ore 17

Caught by a Hurricane 25

August Gale 31

Tug to the Rescue 37

The Most Distressing Wreck 43

Collision 49

Lost with All Hands 53

Fog 61

Lifeboat Disaster 75

War Again 93

Index 103

INTRODUCTION

My interest in shipwrecks began with father's stories of the loss of the Mumbles lifeboat at the wreck of the *Admiral Prinz Adalbert* in 1883, and of the stranding of the *Tours* in 1918. My grandmother, then aged eighteen, was one of the crowd of villagers at the old battery on Mumbles Head who witnessed the capsize of the *Wolverhampton* on that wild Saturday morning one hundred and ten years ago. In the winter and spring of 1918-19 father, then aged seventeen, spent many Sunday afternoons walking from Mumbles to Hunt's Bay to watch the salvage of the steamship *Tours* which was stranded for seven months.

While researching my first book "The Men of the Mumbles Head" (Gomer Press 1977), which told the story of the Mumbles lifeboat station, I began to collect the stories of vessels wrecked on the Gower coast. One might reasonably expect that the two themes of lifeboat and shipwreck were one and the same but this is not so. In the days before the telegraph, telephone and radio many vessels were wrecked unknown to more than a few on the shore. The imperilled crew required immediate assistance from onlookers, it would perhaps be hours before the rescue services (such as existed) could be alerted, by which time it may have been too late to save either life or property.

In the days of sail most of the Gower coast was totally without a lifeboat service and rescue depended on the shipwrecked's own efforts, or the initiative and courage of those who were prepared to launch a boat from the shore. It is true that the coastguard had the use of Manby's line-throwing mortar and later the rocket, but generally these were of use only when the vessel was wrecked on the shore and remained intact long enough to allow the cumbersome apparatus to be got into position.

There have been three lifeboat stations on the Gower coast, those at Mumbles and Port Eynon being well known. The third lifeboat had a brief life but was unique in that it was stationed on a pilot hulk/lightship moored north of Burry Holms in the channel leading to the Burry estuary ports. The lifeboat stationed at Pembrey on the other side of the Burry estuary, also launched to vessels in distress in the Whitford and Burry Holms area. One must not imagine, however, that these lifeboats were able to cover the whole coast. Before 1924, when Mumbles took delivery of its first motor lifeboat, the boats were of very limited range. Their crews did not row them for miles; they were primarily sailing lifeboats, the oars used to leave the shore and to manoeuvre near a wreck. In general too, each station was intended to cover the stretch of coast to leeward since it was practically impossible to make progress against a gale. So the Mumbles lifeboat was intended to launch to casualties in the anchorage at Mumbles Head, and to run before a westerly gale to vessels ashore near Swansea, Port Talbot or the Neath river. Likewise the Port Eynon lifeboat would assist vessels close to the station or run before the wind to casualties at Oxwich and Pennard. Having rescued survivors, the lifeboats landed them at the nearest sheltered spot to leeward; the Mumbles lifeboat often landed crews at Swansea and waited for the weather to moderate before sailing back to its station.

Horatio Tucker began the modern interest in Gower stories with a series of articles in the "South Wales Evening Post" and this culminated in the publication, by the Gower Society in 1951, of his "Gower Gleanings". I had long been puzzled by the chapter "Wrecker's Coast" in this lovely book for it gives little information other than the name and date of a wreck; the circumstances often get no mention. When I was told that Tucker was a nephew of Charles Bevan, hon. secretary of the Port Eynon lifeboat and Lloyd's sub-agent, it began to make sense. Bevan had kept his own record of shipwrecks and seems to have had access to records kept by George Gibbs his predecessor as agent to Lloyd's. Tucker's listing closely follows the material published by Bevan in a letter to "The Cambrian" in 1891.

Of greater value is Jack Beynon's "An Eye-Witness Account of Shipwrecks on the Gower Coast" since the author took part in the rescues as a member of the Rhosili L.S.A. Company. These sources contain inaccuracies in the dates given for certain incidents and these have been perpetuated in some recent books. I have corrected these dates whenever possible, but it would of course be foolish to think that I have not introduced my own errors.

A major disappointment is that I have been unable to put a name to the "dollar wreck" at Rhosili or even to discover the date or circumstance of the loss. This and all the wrecks which occurred before 1804 deserve further attention.

I have ignored the legends concerning shipwreck, most of which were fabricated little more than a century ago. Furthermore one will find no mention of vessels being lured ashore by false lights as such tales also are the product of those ignorant of the sea, and of the realities of navigation. A sufficient illustration is the case of the *Novo Moro*, bound from Lisbon to Amsterdam, which was wrecked on Port Eynon Point at Christmas 1806. Forced by prolonged overcast conditions to estimate his position entirely by dead reckoning, the ship's master believed that he was in the English Channel. This was not an unusual occurrence: many vessels wrecked on the Glamorgan coast and in Carmarthen Bay should have been in the English Channel or sailing up the Irish Sea bound to Liverpool.

SOURCES

Wherever possible I have derived the information from contemporary sources.

The earliest material comes from the manorial records preserved as the Penrice and Margam manuscripts at the National Library of Wales, Aberystwyth.

The letter books of the Swansea Custom House (available at the Public Record Office, Kew) were the source of the eighteenth century material.

Far and away most of the material is derived from local newspapers in particular "The Cambrian" (available at Swansea Museum and Swansea Reference Library) from 1804; the "Cambria Daily Leader" from the 1880s; the "South Wales Daily Post" from 1893 and the "South Wales Evening Post". The newspapers, for most of the period considered, give the most detailed accounts of the wrecks. They also report Board of Trade inquiries where these were held.

Lloyd's Casualty and Loss Books preserved at the Guildhall Library, Aldermanbury, London EC1 have been consulted where the date of a wreck was unknown.

I have also used "Lloyd's List" when searching for information on a particular period. I have consulted this at the Guildhall Library and at the Caird Library of the National Maritime Museum, Greenwich. "Lloyd's Register" has been used to check ship names, tonnages and ports of registry.

ACKNOWLEDGMENTS

My thanks are due to:

Above all, Betty Nelmes M.B.E., for many years administrator of Swansea Museum, for her help, patience and encouragement over more than twenty years.

The present staff of Swansea Museum and of the Maritime and Industrial Museum, Swansea.

The staffs of Swansea Reference Library; West Glamorgan Record Office; the Guildhall Library, London; the library of the National Maritime Museum; the Public Record Office, Kew; and the National Library of Wales.

The late Grahame Farr, of Portishead, the lifeboat and shipping historian, with whom I corresponded for many years.

Michael Gibbs, of Gowerton, for access to a copy of Harriet Gibbs' diary, for his encouragement over many years and for answering numerous questions.

Gerald Gabb, education officer at Swansea's Museums, for drawing my attention to many references in "The Cambrian".

Clive Reid of Derwen Fawr for an account of the wreck of the *Britannia* in 1875.

Tom Thomas of Park Avenue, Mumbles, for information on the *Franklin* and *Seaforth*, and on the rescue of the crew of the *St Christophe* wrecked on Mumbles Head in 1916.

Jim Phillips of Derwen Fawr, for information on the *Ierne*.

ILLUSTRATIONS

The sources of illustrations which accompany the text are individually given but I must acknowledge my indebtedness to those bodies and individuals who have allowed me to reproduce them. The Gower Society, Swansea City Council Leisure Services Dept., World Ship Society (and its members Roy Wilson and Dr Richard Osborne), Walter Jenkins for copies of the Goldsworthy collection of photographs, Gareth Mills, Bernard Morris, Ken Reeves, Michael Gibbs, Robert Lucas and Mrs A. Hughes.

My thanks are also due to Tom Bennett who put me in touch with the owners of some of the photos.

Robert Carl Smith,
Mumbles, 1993

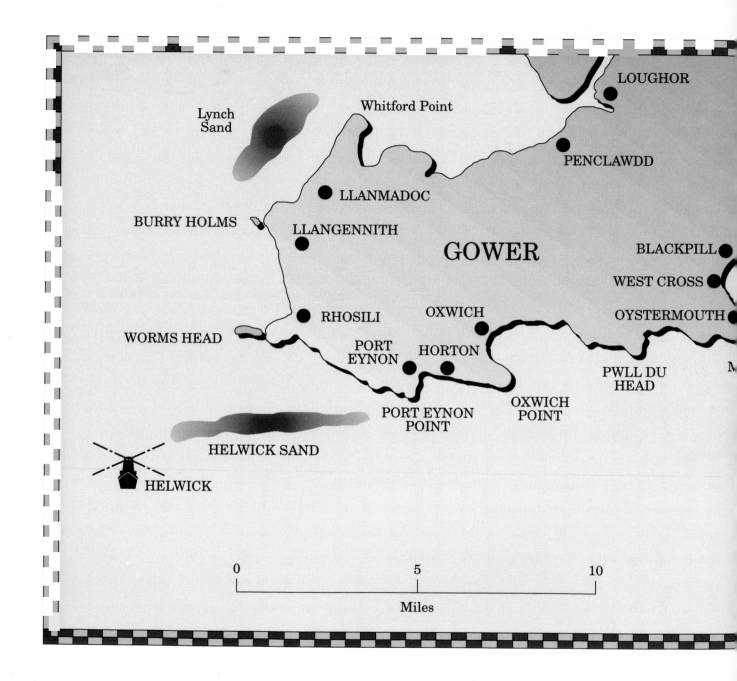

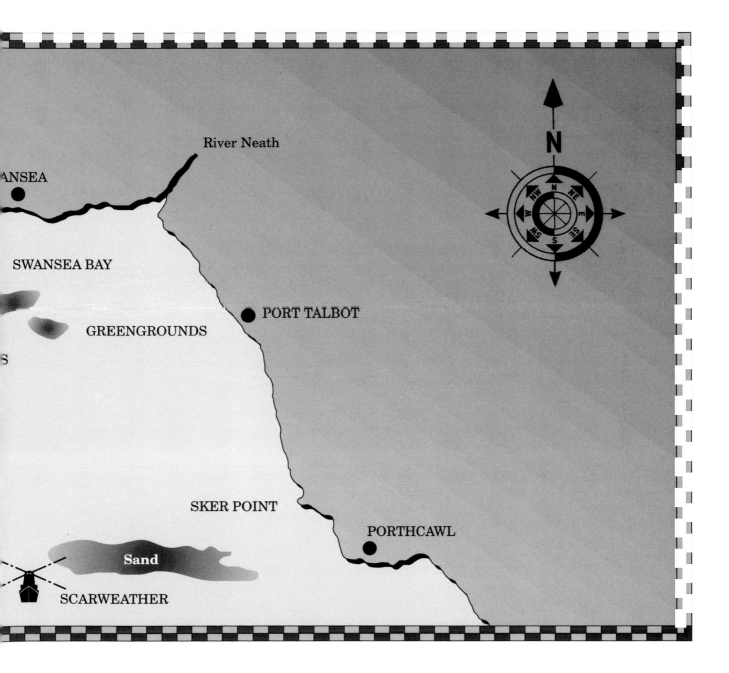

SUGAR, SALT AND ELEPHANT'S TEETH

Accounts of early shipwrecks have usually survived only when rival landowners were in dispute over the ownership of the wrecked vessel and its cargo. The fate of the crew counted for little, the only concern was a quick profit.

A French crayer was driven ashore on Oxwich Point on 26 December 1557. She was probably bound from the Mediterranean to northern France and had been driven too far north to fetch the English Channel. Her crew survived only to be taken prisoner for France and Britain were at war. The vessel's cargo of figs, raisins, almonds and wool was seized by the people of Oxwich under the guidance of the parish priest and the Mansel family of Oxwich Castle who were lords of the manor.

When Sir George Herbert, steward to the Earl of Worcester, heard of the wreck he sent men to the scene to seize it for the crown. When his men returned to Swansea on the morning of the 28th, with the news that the Mansels had already taken the cargo, Herbert set off for Oxwich with a group of horsemen.

There was a brief skirmish between Herbert and Edward Mansel at the gates of Oxwich Castle, but one of Herbert's party then threw a stone into the courtyard striking Anne Mansel, Edward's aunt, on the head. She died of the injury three days later. With the wreck and its crew long forgotten, Edward Mansel's father, Sir Rice, took an action in the court of Star Chamber against Herbert and his men. The case was dealt with on 13 May 1558 and resulted in Herbert and his men being ordered to the Fleet prison until they had paid a fine and restored the seized goods to the Mansels.

Later generations of the same families were again in dispute over a vessel, alleged to be a pirate, which had been driven ashore near Mumbles Head in 1629. The matter was considered by the Attorney General and others, sitting at Hampton Court, who recommended the trial of the survivors "whether they be pirates or not" and the sequestration of the vessel.

In February 1677 (1678 new style), several hogsheads of French wines and many puncheons of brandy, which were washed up at Port Eynon and Oxwich, were taken from the beach for the use of Sir Edward Mansel of Margam. At the same time, the wreckage of a vessel was found on the shore below Pitton cliffs to the east of Rhosili. When it was learnt that Francis Bevan had recovered the vessel's lion figurehead, it too was seized by Edward Mansel's bailiff and sent to Margam.

On a number of occasions in the early nineteenth century coins were recovered from a wreck on Rhosili beach and possibly also from a site at

A dollar of Phillip IV of Spain, minted in Peru, recovered from a ship wrecked on Rhosili beach.

(From H. M. Tucker's Gower Gleanings with permission of the Gower Society)

Bluepool near Burry Holms. The vessel lost on Rhosili beach has been dubbed the "dollar wreck" and coins from it, dated 1625 and 1639, were identified as being dollars of Philip IV of Spain minted at Potosi, Peru. A letter of March 1697/8 from Alexander Trotter, an official of Swansea customs, to Sir Edward Mansel, and which refers to "wreckt iron" and the duty payable on Spanish iron is believed to refer to this wreck. However no information as to the circumstances of the loss or the identity of the vessel has come to light.

On 15 February 1730/31 the Swansea customs reported to London that a vessel had been lost three days earlier near Worms Head, her master and five of the crew surviving. The vessel was driven ashore at the foot of the cliffs below Pilton. She was the *Shepton Mallet*, of Bristol, William Hollier master, homeward bound from Barbadoes with a cargo of 72 hogsheads of sugar, 81 bags of cotton and 204 "elephants teeth". As she was laden with both African and American produce we can assume that she had carried a very different cargo on the "middle passage" between those continents - she was a slaver. The customs reported that 53 of the tusks had been recovered and were secured under the King's lock, but that the rest had been carried off by the country people. Some days passed before the landwaiter and two tidesmen were sent to search houses and farms in the area. The commissioners ordered copies of the following notice to be printed, read to the population of surrounding areas and "fixed up in ye most publick places":

"This is to give notice to all persons concerned in taking away and concealing or receiving any of the Elephants Teeth, or other goods salved out of the *Shepton Mallet*, of Bristol, lately stranded near Port Inon that if they do not forthwith bring the said goods to the Custom house warehouse, or to Mr Caleb Thomas at Pitton, that they will be prosecuted as the law directs."

Matthew Price, the officer at Oxwich, reported that several people who had salvaged cotton from the wreck had refused to take it to the warehouse "under the pretence of not having been paid for securing it".

On 16 January 1746/7 the *Nieuwe Goude Spoor*, Jansen Vlenget master, from Essequibo (Guiana) for Middelburg (Holland) with over 700 hogsheads of sugar, cocoa nuts and limejuice, drove from her anchors in Mumbles roads and went ashore at Brynmill. Discharging of the vessel began immediately, and the cargo soon filled a number of warehouses in Swansea. Spring tides damaged the hull, but the vessel was refloated and got into harbour for repairs on 17 February.

Another vessel successfully refloated was the *Charming Nancy*, of Cork, John Reardon master. Bound from Lisbon with a cargo of salt and fruit she stranded near Mumbles Head on 16 December 1748. The salvage account has survived in the customs records and shows that Able Clement and George Robbins used their sloops to unload the cargo, while Philip Powell recovered her anchors and was paid £2-1s-6d. A little over £10 was paid for the attendance of the customs officers, John Pritchard was paid £2-12s-8d for the repairs carried out at Mumbles, and Henry Squire claimed £6-16s for the repairs he completed after the vessel had been taken into harbour on 8 January. James Griffiths, who oversaw the salvage operation, was paid 10 guineas, and ale for the sixteen labourers cost eighteen shillings and nine pence.

Two other vessels lost their cables when

anchored in Mumbles roads and drove onto the mud flats, losing their masts as they grounded. The *Two Sisters*, with salt and fruit from St Ubes (Portugal) for Dram (Holland) went ashore on 31 January 1749/50. Three days later she was followed by the *Eagle*, James Thompson master, with fruit and bale goods from Genoa for London. On her voyage the *Eagle* had been captured by an Algerine man-of-war which had taken her mate and five men, replacing them with six of her own. Capt Thompson had been ordered to steer for Algiers but had lost sight of his captors during darkness and put into St Lucar, near Cadiz, to land the pirates. The masters of both vessels were allowed to sell the perishable parts of their cargoes to pay for repairs.

"Lloyd's List" for 5 December 1760 carried the item: "The *Caesar*, Bristol to Plymouth, has been lost to the west of Mumbles; 62 men and 3 women perished". This shipwreck has fascinated Gower folk for generations but the details were sketchy until Walter Jenkins researched the events and published an account in vol. 26 of *Gower* (the journal of the Gower Society). With his permission, and that of the society, the following relies heavily on that account. The *Caesar* and *Reeves*, merchant ships requisitioned for naval service, were carrying impressed men from Bristol to Plymouth. The *Caesar* was manned by her usual civilian crew with her master, Adam Drake, taking his orders from Lt. James Gaborian who, in turn, took his orders from the lieutenant of the *Reeves* . The vessels left Mumbles roads, where they had been sheltering, on the morning of Friday 28 November using the ebb tide to help them down channel. When the tide began to make, the vessels met worsening weather and the lieutenant of the *Reeves* signalled a return to Mumbles. By 4 p.m. the crew of the *Caesar* made

out a headland on the port bow and another on the port beam. William Barry, pilot of the vessel, told Capt Drake that he would take her back to Mumbles, though the master was in favour of anchoring off shore. At 4.30 Drake ordered the lead to be used and bottom was found in 13 fathoms. A little later they were in 10 fathoms. Once again Drake wanted to anchor while Barry was confident of gaining the anchorage. The mate, Thomas Lammas, was on the forecastle keeping a sharp lookout and at 5 p.m. shouted "breakers ahead!". The crew attempted to get off the land by wearing ship, but the manoeuvre did not succeed and the vessel was soon tearing her bilges out on the rocks of Pwll Du Point. The lieutenant, Drake and more than sixty men escaped from the vessel. The bodies recovered from the wreck, mainly those of the impressed men kept prisoner below deck, were buried in a mass grave on the eastern slope of the headland at a spot known to this day as Gravesend. The gulley where the vessel was wrecked is similarly called Caesar's Hole.

The brigantine *Friendship*, George Gilbert master, was driven ashore "on backside of Whiteford Burrows" on 10 November 1767 with the loss of two of her crew. The 190 ton vessel, was bound from Philadelphia to Bristol, with a cargo which included 52 tons of pig iron, 3,000 deerskins, 90 pieces of mahogany and cedar, 4 hogsheads of rum, a cask of snake root and 37 barrels of turpentine. Capt Gilbert set up camp on the dunes and got the cargo discharged. George Watson, the merchant to whom the cargo was consigned, hired a sloop to take the salvaged goods to Bristol. Though the hull had now sunk in the sand and was full of water, Capt Gilbert hoped to refloat it using empty barrels. The following April the *Eagle*, Capt Hovey, bound from

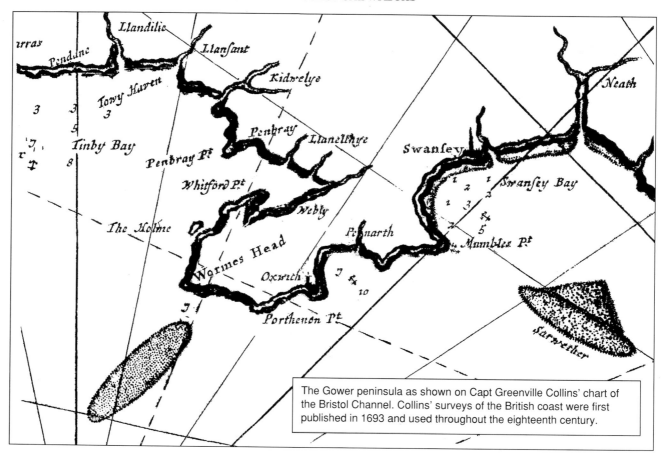

The Gower peninsula as shown on Capt Greenville Collins' chart of the Bristol Channel. Collins' surveys of the British coast were first published in 1693 and used throughout the eighteenth century.

Pisagua (Chile) for Bristol, was also wrecked at Whitford.

The Padstow sloop *Seaflower* foundered off Pwll Du on Sunday 7 July 1776. The body of her master, Thomas Retallick, was cast ashore at Oxwich the following Thursday and lies buried in the churchyard.

In October 1780 the *Charlotte*, Codd master, bound from Bristol to Cork, went ashore at Mumbles though her fate is not recorded, and in November 1782 the *Endeavour*, Morgan master, with a cargo of copper ore from Hayle to Swansea, drove ashore and was wrecked on Oxwich Point.

The ship *Saetia Mazzed* was captured by the *Stag*, letter of marque of Liverpool, in July 1783 and condemned as a prize. On 10 January the following year the vessel drove ashore at Llangennith and was wrecked. Part of her cargo of brandy and elephant tusks, which was consigned to William Jones of Swansea, was looted by the "country people".

In August 1785 the *Leverpool*, Bristol bound, was run down off Worms Head by a Swansea bound vessel and five of the crew were drowned.

On the evening of Friday 23 July 1790 one of the Swansea pilot boats capsized off Mumbles Head drowning the pilot, his son and three assistants; and in December that year the *Resolution*, Williams master, London to Barnstaple, foundered off the Worm with the loss of all hands.

"Lloyd's List" for 6 March 1792 reflected the Gower man's difficulty with the pronunciation of Welsh place names, with the item: "The *Lovely Betsey* is lost in Pool Day bay near Swansea".

The *Hayle Trader*, Capt Hamley, Bristol to Hayle, foundered off Mumbles Head in November 1793; whether the crew survived is not recorded.

In March 1794, the sloop *Eliza*, Vaughan master, bound from Bridgwater to Liverpool, was lost with all hands on the Mixon sandbank which lies just to the west of Mumbles Head.

Swansea Harbour Trust had been formed in 1791 and by May 1794 had built Mumbles Lighthouse. At first it was lit by two coal fires, but five years later an oil lamp and reflectors were installed. The light greatly improved the safety of the approaches to Swansea and to the important anchorage at Mumbles by indicating the position of the Mixon shoal. Fog and copper smoke from the numerous smelters at Swansea naturally reduced its effectiveness at times, but the loom of the light still sweeps the channel every night.

On 19 January 1796 the Collector of Customs at Swansea wrote to the Board in London reporting the loss of the brigantine *Priscilla* , of Dartmouth, a few days previously. The vessel, bound from Bristol to Alderney with barrel staves, bottles, candles, soap and tar, had driven ashore under Pilton cliffs and went to pieces. A part of the cargo had been recovered and was held by the customs and by Thomas Mansel Talbot as lord of the manor. The collector finished his report by writing: "It is feared that the crew has perished; a cat was the only living thing on board".

The *Sisters*, Borlase master, bound from St Ives to Neath, went down with all hands off the Worm in November 1797.

The Port Eynon burial register contains the following entry under 27 June 1802: "John Cutliffe, mariner, of Coomb St Martin, Devon, drowned about six weeks since, his vessel foundering in Rhosili Bay. His corpse ashore on this beach this morning, and identified by his name engraved on the case of his watch. His uncle, then at Swansea, recognising it". No ship losses in the area are recorded during May 1802, but "Lloyd's List" for 9 March records that the *Neptune*, Barnstaple to Bristol, had been lost "on the Welsh coast" drowning her crew of seven.

Being the parish church of a seaport, St Mary's, Swansea, contained numerous memorials of maritime interest. The church was gutted by incendiary bombs during the last war but many of the inscriptions had been recorded. One of interest here, was the memorial to Joseph Peters, of Padstow, a twenty two year old master mariner drowned when his vessel was wrecked in Oxwich Bay on 20 November 1802. Peters' body was recovered and buried at St Mary's. The memorial inscription carried the lines:

" 'Twas thine dear youth to find an early grave
   To fly from time and future worlds explore
   To suffer shipwreck on the northern wave
   And lie entomb'd upon a distant shore."

COAL AND COPPER ORE

The year 1804 opened with a "tremendous gale of wind" which drove a number of vessels ashore at Mumbles, but all were got off with little damage. At the other end of the peninsula, the sloop *Two Sisters*, of Padstow, George Hawker master, was wrecked near Whitford Point. Her cargo of 50 tons of rag slates from the Delabole quarry (Cornwall) was sold by auction at John Bevan's public house at Frog Lane, Llanmadoc, on 16 February.

On the night of 23 April that year the sloop *Unity*, Portreath to Neath with copper ore, struck the Mixon in a strong gale. With huge seas sweeping over her she soon broke up drowning Capt Walker and his crew of two. The wreckage came ashore at Broadslade (now known as Bracelet) Bay, from where the more useful parts quickly vanished.

Another heavy gale on 5 November drove vessels from their anchors in Mumbles roads. Several were damaged, but the only serious casualty was the brig *Recovery*, Cardiff to Falmouth with coal. She sank in the shallows but dried at low water. Lt. Garret and the crew of H. M. brig *Endeavour*, on convoy duty because of the war, assisted to discharge her cargo and raise the vessel. Two days earlier, a loaded smuggling vessel had run into the roads to seek shelter, but seeing the *Endeavour* and another armed brig, the *Morriston*, along with the custom and impress cutters, she had quickly tacked and stood down channel under a press of sail - the authorities had no chance of catching her!

The *Fanny*, Capt Salter, Neath to Cork with a cargo of culm, stranded on Skysea on the night of 22 June 1805. With the vessel breaking up the crew abandoned and rowed ashore at Port Eynon; and on Boxing Day that year the Swansea sloop *Rose* struck on Port Eynon Point. Labourer Thomas Hopkin saw a man struggling in the water and, at the risk of his own life, dashed in to drag seaman John Stephens ashore. The sloop's master, Sam Davies, his son and two others were drowned.

On the night of 4 June 1806 a vessel was lost with all hands on the Mixon. It was some days before she was identified as the sloop *Hope*, Reed master, bound from Tenby to Bridgwater.

The ship *Novo Moro* sailed from Lisbon on 1 December 1806 bound to Amsterdam with a cargo which included cotton, sugar, fruit, wine, coconuts and hides. Three weeks later her master, Joye de Santos d'Olivera, was unsure of his position due to prolonged overcast weather. Hoping to make landfall at the Lizard on the south coast of Cornwall, he had lookouts posted. His troubles increased when a

---

A CARD.

JOHN PAWSON, *Master of the Recovery Brig, of Falmouth, which sunk at the Mumbles on Monday the 5th of November, begs leave to present his grateful thanks to Lieutenant Garrett, and the Ship's Crew, of his Majesty's Armed-Brig, Endeavour, for their very friendly and spirited exertions in raising his vessel, to which he entirely attributes her being saved from destruction.*

The brig *Recovery* sank at Mumbles during a heavy gale on 5 November 1804. Her cargo of coal was discharged and she was refloated with the assistance of the crew of the armed brig *Endeavour*. ('The Cambrian', Swansea Museum)

TO BE SOLD BY AUCTION,

On Friday, the 6th day of February next, at the Brewery, on the Strand, in the town of Swansea, the under-mentioned Articles, being PART of the CARGO of the SHIP MORO, viz.

A QUANTITY of PORTUGAL WOOL.
20 BAGS of ARCHELIA WEED.
5 BAGS of COTTON.
80 BUFFALO HIDES.

And on Monday, the 16th of February, will be SOLD. the remaining part of the MATERIALS of the said SHIP, consisting of SAILS, JUNK, CORDAGE, ANCHORS, a LARGE BOAT, with sundry other articles.

The sale will commence each day at eleven o'clock.

For particulars, apply at the Counting-house of William Grove and Son, on the Strand.

The ship *Novo Moro* was bound from Lisbon to Amsterdam when she was wrecked at Port Eynon on Christmas Day 1806. (*'The Cambrian'*, Swansea Museum)

seaman fell to his death from the main t'gallant yard. Two days later, during the early hours of Christmas Day, the ship struck on Port Eynon Point ripping open her bottom. The master and crew, nineteen all told, took to the longboat but, hearing the surf thundering on the shore, they wisely ran before the wind to find a sheltered bay in which to land. A few hours later they reached the safety of Mumbles. The vessel became a complete wreck and scattered her cargo over Port Eynon Bay, requiring numerous customs officers and labourers to recover it under the supervision of William Grove, the Swansea merchant and Portuguese vice-consul, who acted for the owners. What remained was auctioned at the brewery, Swansea, on 6 February 1807. Ten days later the sails, anchors and other materials of the wreck came under the hammer, but it was to be August that year before the nine casks of white wine, which had also been saved, were auctioned, on behalf of the customs, by Simon Llewelyn

who is remembered to this day as the man who ran a passenger service on the Mumbles railway. In a letter to the Board of Customs, the collector at Swansea had reported that the wine "being of the growth of Portugal, thin and not of a pleasant flavour" had an estimated value "much below the duties payable". The salvage meeting was opened at the Mackworth Arms, Swansea, on 6 March 1807 to receive the claims of those who took part in saving the cargo. It was held before three magistrates: Rev. John Collins, William Jones and John Jones, whose task it was to consider and adjust each claim. The total cost of salvage amounted to £1,308-7s-3d.

The big spring tides of February 1807 exposed the "dollar wreck" at Rhosili and about twelve pounds weight of coin was recovered. On 24 March William Weston Young, of Porthcawl, whose business interests included the salvage of wrecks and their cargoes, visited Rhosili and agreed to work on "Hancorne's wreck" for a half share: Samuel Hancorne was the Collector of Customs at Swansea. On 17 April, Young sent a cart of materials to Rhosili and went there himself on the 20th. The next day D. Beynon took him to the "dollar wreck" but whether Young worked on it is not clear.

The Carmarthen sloop *Brothers*, Matthew Yetman master, bound from her home port to Bristol with oats, butter and eggs, was driven ashore near Burry Holms on Saturday 11 April 1807. Her crew and passengers were saved "with great difficulty" before the vessel went to pieces.

The Preventive Water Guard was formed in 1809 to combat smuggling. Britain was divided into thirty one districts each led by an inspecting commander. The stations at Mumbles and Port Eynon each had an officer, chief boatman and boat's crew armed with carbines, muskets, pistols, bayonets and cutlasses. More importantly they also had a six-oared galley and Manby's line-throwing mortar for use at a wreck. In 1822 the Water Guard became H.M. Coastguard.

The Mixon claimed another victim in the shape of the *Friendship*, Capt Rees, with Irish copper ore for Swansea, in the early hours of 26 February 1810. The crew abandoned and got ashore safely.

Late on the evening of 9 November 1810, a sou'westerly gale backed to south-east and caught a number of vessels sheltering at Mumbles. The *Lord Nelson*, Howells master, with navy timber from Chepstow to Plymouth, struck bottom and was badly damaged, and the *Britannia*, Capt Peters, Swansea to Waterford with coal, sank at her anchors. No lives were lost and the *Britannia* was discharged, raised and put up for sale the following April.

When the sloop *Elizabeth*, of Castlehaven, stranded on the banks off Whitford in January 1811, help was at hand in the shape of Tom Prance, the customs boat-sitter, and John Morgan the tide-waiter. They succeeded in raising the vessel and got her to Penclawdd for repair.

The Swansea brig *Nancy*, Roberts master, foundered off Worms Head with the loss of all hands in April 1811.

The *Brothers*, John Dalton master, was abandoned in a sinking condition near Lundy while bound to Swansea with copper ore and timber in November 1812. The crew drifted north in their boat and were picked up by a vessel in Carmarthen Bay. The *Brothers* remained afloat and drifted ashore west of Oxwich Point where she went to pieces; much of her cargo was salvaged.

On Wednesday 8 September 1813, the 30 ton Ilfracombe sloop *Ann & Sarah*, with a cargo of coal from Llanelli, sprang a leak while crossing Rhosili Bay. The vessel sank as she was being run for the shore. The master, James Irwin, climbed the rigging while the two crew members took to the boat which capsized as they were going ashore. The boy was drowned but the man grasped an oar which kept him afloat. Struggling ashore, he raised the alarm and local men Moses Gibb, John Thomas and William Harry launched their boat and rescued the master after he had spent many hours on the mast.

In October 1815 three men were drowned in Oxwich Bay when their boat capsized as they dredged for oysters. One was George Ace of Oxwich whose grave may still be seen in the churchyard.

The *Elizabeth*, of Portsmouth, had sailed from Swansea with a cargo of coal when contrary winds forced her back. She struck the Mixon on 3 August 1817, was refloated, but sank before she could be run ashore.

The peninsula was swept by a heavy sou'westerly gale late on the evening of Wednesday 17 December 1817. The next morning John Prosser, Inspecting Commander of District 15 of the Water Guard, was at the Port Eynon station when the watch came down from the lookout to report a wreck on Oxwich Point. Prosser immediately accompanied Edward Bartlett, the station officer, and the seven men of his crew, under arms, to the scene. Having dispersed the "intoxicated population", who had already got at the cargo, they assisted Francis Bevan, the coast officer at Oxwich, to secure what remained and recovered about three hundred gallons of brandy and gin. This was placed under the guard of the preventive men until it could be taken to Swansea as "a number of persons from the country had collected with an evident design of plunder". The wreck was of the smack *La Manche*, of Morlaix, a smuggler of only about 20 tons burthen. The spirits were in "small casks, ready slung with small cordage for a run on some part of the coast". Three bodies came ashore and on that of the master, Guillaume, was a letter in French addressed to someone living in Dartmouth. The vessel's manifest was also found and showed that her cargo had been 130 four gallon casks intended for customers in Devon.

The brig *Bounty Hall*, of Liverpool, John Roberts master, was homeward bound from Calcutta with a valuable cargo which included teak planks, tobacco, borax, cotton, rice, sugar, saltpetre, galingale, munjeet and ginger. Thick weather caused the 370 ton vessel to lose her course and strand at Whitford on the night of 19 December 1819. Tom Prance, the armless boat-sitter, and the crew of the Whitford customs boat were joined by Bartlett and the preventive men from Port Eynon. With George Holland, Lloyd's agent, living nearby at Cwm Ivy, the master had all the assistance he required to save his ship. Holland informed his brother John, who lived at Kilvrough, and he sent word to the magistrates. A troop of the Swansea Cavalry was sent down to guard the cargo which had been unloaded onto the sand dunes and covered with tarpaulins. The sugar and saltpetre were ruined but the rest was little damaged. The brig was first got into Whitford Pill and then towed up to Penclawdd. After repairs, the *Bounty Hall* reloaded her cargo and sailed for home in the last week of February 1820.

Two small craft were lost in Rhosili Bay on 21 January 1820. The *John*, of Padstow, foundered during the morning drowning her crew of two men and a boy; the body of John Slocombe, her master, was found and buried at Rhosili church. A few

hours later the *George*, Sincock master, with copper ore for Llanelli was wrecked near the Worm. Two of the crew leapt ashore as she struck the rocks, but the master and a seaman took to the rigging. Word was sent to Port Eynon and, in the absence of the water guard who were attending the *Bounty Hall*, Sam Gibbs arrived with the Manby line-throwing mortar. Charles Steel, Inspecting Commander of the Water Guard, assisted by the crew of the preventive boat, put the apparatus to good effect and saved the two. (In January 1841 Steel, now commander of the coastguard at St Mary's, Isles of Scilly, won the gold medal of the Lifeboat Institution for his gallantry in saving survivors from the paddle steamer *Thames* wrecked on the Western Rocks.)

A Lynmouth smack capsized and sank, with the loss of three members of her crew of four, on the morning of 2 August 1820 while dredging for oysters off Port Eynon. Six weeks later, the Cardigan sloop *Diligence*, bound to Bristol with a cargo of oats, was driven ashore and wrecked near Worms Head; her crew survived.

The Swansea sloop *Trafalgar* left port on the morning of 12 September 1821 with copper ore for Llanelli. The next morning she was off the Worm when she was caught in a strong gale and foundered. The master, John Bevan, and his crewman abandoned in the boat but were severely bruised on the rocks as they got ashore.

A full-size male figure-head was found at Oxwich in the first week of January 1822. Sacks of flour and coffee beans were also washed up but the identity of the wreck was not discovered. A month later the sloop *Sally & William*, Rose master, was driven ashore in Oxwich Bay by a violent gale.

The Chichester sloop *Appledram*, George

Gauntlett master, in ballast for Swansea, was driven ashore just to the east of Worms Head in a gale on 16 May 1823. The master and crew were put up at Rhosili while the Swansea shipwrights Meager and Richards worked on the vessel. The whole village turned out to cheer when the sloop was refloated on the evening tide of 6 June.

As the Swansea pilot boat *Angally* ran alongside a vessel three miles south-west of Mumbles Head on 27 June 1823 she was run down and sunk. Pilot Bevan jumped aboard the vessel, but his two assistants spent a long time in the water before being picked up.

A rare north-easterly storm with snow squalls drove the Whitehaven brig *Hero* from her anchors in Mumbles roads on 30 October 1823. The vessel sank near the lighthouse and Meager and Richards were once again called in. They succeeded in raising the vessel just five days later. In the following month Mumbles lighthouse was modernised when the London firm of Robinson and Wilkins installed improved lamps and reflectors.

On Monday 22 November 1824, over one hundred vessels were sheltering at Mumbles from a sou'westerly gale. In the evening the wind backed to south-east and blew a near hurricane with rain and thunder. There was considerable confusion as vessels parted their cables and drove through the anchorage. Fourteen were driven ashore with the loss of masts, yards and bowsprits. All except the Falmouth schooner *Lavinia* and a Bideford sloop were refloated.

In the last week of January 1825 large quantities of oats came ashore at Llangennith along with several pieces of timber. The sloop *Menai*, of Newport (Pembs.), had gone down off Rhosili with the loss of all hands.

The Swansea pilot boat *Friends* sailed from the port on the ebb tide on 8 November 1825. A southwest gale was blowing and a fleet of coasters was known to be in the offing. Having put pilot Deusbury aboard a vessel, the boat was "returning too early on the tide, and keeping too near the shore" when she shipped a succession of seas and foundered drowning the assistant Sam Hopkins and two boys. The next day the gale shifted to the north and increased in force. Ten vessels, including the Barmouth smack *Bonny Kate*, were driven ashore at Mumbles, while the brig *Ponsonby*, of Cork, with coal from Newport, sank at her anchors. The brig's cargo was discharged at low water, and she was taken into Swansea where repairs were carried out on the patent slip. It was to be another ten months before she would resume her voyage.

The *Union*, a fine new 300 ton brig, was making down channel on passage to Jersey when the wind swung to the west. Capt Perchard decided to bear up for Mumbles on the evening of 10 April 1826. In the haze they failed to sight Mumbles light and struck the Mixon. The vessel filled at once forcing the crew to abandon ship and seek refuge on a vessel anchored in the roads.

Fog was the undoing of the sloop *Three Brothers*, of Barnstaple, Huxtable master, Hayle to Swansea with copper ore, which ran ashore near Oxwich Point on 20 March 1827. The crew got ashore and, although the vessel became a complete wreck, much of the cargo was recovered.

A cargo of sheep came to a sad end on the night of 4 May 1827. The sloop *Atlas*, of New Ross, bound to Swansea, ran ashore at Llanmadoc. She filled at once drowning all but six of the one hundred and five animals. Local men John Bevan and Dick Richards assisted the crew ashore.

The Bideford brigantine *George* was bound home from Bristol on the morning of 14 February 1828, when she was caught by a violent south-easter. Course was changed for Swansea, but at about 2 a.m. as she approached, her crew mistook a light on shore for that at the harbour entrance. The vessel struck the beach and filled. With the tide making, and a heavy sea running, the crew took to the rigging remaining there for two hours before rescue from the shore. Later that day seven local men were engaged to salvage the vessel's materials, but they found a jar of whisky and were soon incapable of work. Two were in such a state that tackles had to be rigged to lift them from the hold. They were carried home on ladders and doctors called to administer the stomach pump!

When the sloop *Speculator* capsized and sank off Mumbles Head during a gale on 9 August 1828, the crew were picked up by the 200 ton steam packet *Palmerston*, John Hyde commander, which ran the regular Bristol to Swansea service. The sloop *Seaflower*, of Bannow (Co. Wexford), Wilman master, was anchored at Rhosili sheltering from the gale when her cables parted. Her crew got ashore when she struck the beach but the sloop then went to pieces. Three days later the *William & Mary*, of Plymouth, Slocombe master, bound to Neath with copper ore foundered in Oxwich Bay. Her crew also got ashore safely.

At 4 o'clock on the afternoon of 10 October 1828, a brig in a sinking condition was seen standing in for the shore near Burry Holms. The vessel sank, before those watching could go to her assistance. She was identified by her boat, which went ashore at Rhosili, as the *Juno*, of St Ives. The two bodies recovered were identified by men from Llanelli, where the brig was a regular trader, as those of

James Kempstone, the master, and Charles Richards: "they have since been decently buried, side by side, in Llangennith churchyard" reported "The Cambrian". The Admiralty survey of the Bristol Channel was then in progress under the direction of Lt. H. M. Denham R.N. in H.M.S. *Shamrock*. Denham had found that the Helwick sandbank extended further west than existing charts showed, and it was conjectured that the *Juno* had struck the western end of the bank.

The sloop *Jane*, of St Clears, William Jordan master, was on passage from Bristol to Carmarthen with a cargo of freestone and shop goods. During the night of 4 November 1828 she sprang a leak and the master ran the vessel for the shore. The water gained so fast that they were forced to abandon her, and she drifted onto the rocks about a mile east of Worms Head. The next morning the crew were joined by the customs in saving what they could of the cargo.

The *Lively*, of Sunderland, with iron from Cardiff, sank on the Mixon on the morning of 16 October 1829. The master, mate and boy were swept to their deaths. Three survivors spent some hours in the rigging before being saved by the

---

NOTICE.

ALL Persons having PICKED UP any of the WRECK of the BRIG LIVELY, of Sunderland, lately lost near the Mumble Head, are requested to give Notice, or deliver the same, to Mr. John Richardson, Ship-Owner, Swansea, who is duly authorised by the Underwriter to receive and dispose of the same, and pay the lawful Salvage to the Parties saving the said Wreck; and any Person found secreting any of the Stores or Materials belonging to this Vessel, will be dealt with according to law.

When the brig *Lively* was wrecked on the Mixon sandbank in October 1829, her master, mate and boy were swept to their deaths. Three survivors were rescued by a Swansea pilot boat. (*'The Cambrian'*, Swansea Museum)

Swansea pilot boat *Sarah*, Herbert Blackmore master.

The brig *Idas*, of Whitby, with a cargo of timber from Miramichi (New Brunswick) for Gloucester, went ashore at Langland during thick fog at 6.30 on the morning of Wednesday 9 December 1829. She became a complete wreck but her cargo was salvaged and sold by auction.

On 23 June 1830 the *Irish Miners*, of Cardigan, carrying copper ore from Swansea to Llanelli, was wrecked when she struck the Dangers reef which lies to the east of Worms Head. Coastguard officer Bartlett and his men saved the master, David Nicholas, and his crew.

Later that year another vessel fell foul of the sandbanks while trying to work into the Burry Estuary. The brig *Henry*, of Harrington (Nova Scotia), Quebec to Penclawdd with timber, stranded off Whitford on the morning of 29 October. She was badly damaged but her cargo kept her afloat allowing crew and passengers to get ashore. The passengers were the crew of the London ship *Hibbert* which the *Henry* had found waterlogged and on her beam ends in mid Atlantic. The *Hibbert*'s men had clung to the side of the vessel for three days with little food or water and were very lucky to have survived. When they got to Swansea, the *Hibbert's* crew were given a free passage to Bristol by Capt Hyde of the *Palmerston*.

The sloop *Ilfracombe Packet* grounded while entering Swansea on a stormy day in February 1832. She got broadside to the shore and her crew were in considerable danger. Two boats of hobblers failed to get near, but five pilots led by Silvanus Padley, son of the clerk to the Harbour Trust, then went out with a spare anchor and cable. They boarded the sloop, got her bows to the seas, kedged

> **To Timber Merchants, Masters of Vessels,**
> *&c. &c.*
>
> **TO BE SOLD BY AUCTION,**
> By LLEWELYN & BOWEN,
> (By order and for account of the Importers), on WEDNESDAY, the 13th of JANUARY, 1830, precisely at eleven o'clock in the forenoon, in LANGLAND BAY,
> PART of the CARGO saved from the Wreck of the BRIG IDUS, bound from Miramichi to Gloucester, WM. HILL RAMSDEN, Master; consisting of about 300 Pieces of Red and Yellow Pine Deals and Lathwood, in lots to suit purchasers.
> Also, PART of the STORES of the said Brig, left unsold, consisting of Chain Cables, Anchors, Hawsers, Boats, Yards, Rigging, &c.
> NOTICE.—Any person found pilfering Part of the above Wreck, will be prosecuted; and a REWARD of FIVE GUINEAS will be given, on such information as may lead to conviction, by the Master on the spot, or at the Counting-House of Messrs. Wm. Grove and Son, Merchants, Swansea, who will also give any particulars required as to the Sale.

The brig *Idas*, of Whitby, was wrecked at Langland in December 1829. (*'The Cambrian'*, Swansea Museum)

her off and finally warped the vessel and her crew into harbour. The pilots were voted cash rewards and the Trust decided to explore the possibility of obtaining a lifeboat for the port.

Later that year the people of Mumbles and district met at the Mermaid Inn to consider setting up a lifeboat station to protect the crews of vessels which sought shelter in the roads. The meeting was chaired by Tom Prance of Penclawdd, the customs boat-sitter and former merchant skipper, who had lost both hands many years before when his vessel had been attacked by a French privateer. It was to be another three years before a lifeboat actually arrived at Mumbles, and even then the station proved to be quite ineffective until transferred to the Lifeboat Institution in 1863. In any case such a lifeboat would have been of use only in the roads or western part of Swansea Bay; it could not have served the south or west coasts of the peninsula.

CAUGHT BY A HURRICANE

After nearly three weeks of bad weather, masters of windbound vessels were glad to see Tuesday 19 February 1833 dawn with a "serene sky and a light easterly breeze". Many vessels sailed from Swansea with coal for ports in Devon and Cornwall. During the evening, however, the wind veered to south and was soon blowing a strong gale as it swung to south-west. At 5 a.m. on Wednesday, the wind shifted to north-west and blew at hurricane force for the rest of the day. Vessels which were in mid channel put about to seek shelter at Mumbles. The smack *Surprise*, of Clovelly, with 20 tons of culm for Bude, reached Swansea Bay leaking badly and sank before she could be run ashore. Her crew abandoned and were picked up by another vessel. The Padstow schooner *Frances Anne*, with coal for St Ives, foundered near the Greengrounds off Mumbles with the loss of her crew of six and four passengers. William Weston Young of Neath worked on the vessels for two months and successfully raised them. During the same storm a schooner was seen to founder on the Helwick; her masts came ashore at Oxwich but she was not identified. At Port Eynon there was a double tragedy: the Campletown schooner *Favourite*, and the sloop *Mary*, of Laugharne, were driven ashore and lost with all hands. The *Mary* had been returning from Bristol with groceries for St Clears; tobacco, gin and vinegar were found amongst the debris.

When the Maryport brig *Amethyst*, Quebec to Liverpool, lost her rudder in an Atlantic storm she drifted up channel and stranded on Swansea beach on 28 November 1833. Pilot John Mitchell was quickly on the scene in his boat *William IV* to save Capt Hodgson and the crew of ten. The National Institution for the Preservation of Life from Shipwreck, as the Lifeboat Institution was then called, made an award of £5 to be divided between Mitchell and his crew of three. The brig was refloated to the west pier by the Swansea shipwright John Richardson allowing her cargo of flour, wheat and pearl ashes to be discharged.

The London brig *Syren* left Swansea on 18 December with coal for the government steamers at Malta. She ran into a gale off the Worm, became unmanageable, and was driven ashore near Burry Holms. Her crew got ashore in the boat, but the vessel broke up so quickly that within a few hours parts of it were found at Loughor.

The "dollar wreck" was once again exposed in January 1834 and more coins, pewter and iron were recovered by local people. Some reports say that cannon and part of an astrolabe were also found. At Glamorgan Assizes in March 1835 C.R.M. Talbot, lord of the manor, sought to establish his right to the wrecks in Rhosili Bay. He was awarded one shilling damages against "Lewis and others" which established his manorial right.

The barque *Margaret*, of Malta, sailed from Swansea on 1 November 1834 with coal for Ali Pacha's steam boats at Alexandria. Five days out, a storm brought down the fore and main yards and the seas got below. She put back for Milford but, finding it hazy as she neared the haven, course was shaped for Mumbles. The vessel was anchored south-east of the lighthouse but struck bottom at low water. Leaving most of his hands at the pumps, the master was rowed to Swansea where Capt William Moyse, Lloyd's agent, arranged tugs which beached the barque at Oystermouth.

Nine days later, on 17 November, the schooner *Mary Ann*, of Wexford, bound home with coal from Cardiff, gave up the struggle against headwinds but struck the Mixon as she made for Mumbles. Crew and passengers landed safely, and on the next ebb Lt. Alldridge, station officer of Mumbles coastguard, and his men boarded the wreck to recover stores before it went to pieces.

At 1.30 a.m. on 22 October 1835 the brig *New Blessing*, Cardiff to Waterford, struck the Cardigan ketch *Heart of Oak* which was lying to and showing no lights midway between Lundy and Worms Head. The brig lost her bowsprit and foremast and drifted up to a point near the Helwick where she was anchored. The crew then found that she was leaking badly and abandoned shortly before she went down.

On the evening of Wednesday 12 October 1836, a storm blew which exceeded in fury anything that even the oldest inhabitant could remember. The brig *Cobrero*, with coal for Cuba, lost her foremast when run foul of by a schooner drifting through the anchorage at Mumbles. Later in the night, the schooner *Success*, of Fowey, had difficulty weighing anchor. The mate and two men launched the boat to assist but it was capsized drowning them. The bodies of William Hicks, Henry Ellery and sixteen year old Jonathan Ellery were recovered and buried in Oystermouth churchyard where the stone which marked their grave may still be seen bearing the lines:

"If youth or strength our lives could save
And keep us from a watery grave
This lonesome stone would not be found
To tell alas that we were drown'd
And in a moment snatched away
From shades of night to realms of day"

The *Petersburgh*, of Milford, Quebec to Llanelli with timber, was anchored off Burry bar on the afternoon of 7 December 1836 awaiting the tide. The westerly wind freshened and she parted her chains and drove onto the Lynch sandbank. The crew abandoned and got ashore safely. The vessel's cargo kept her intact and she was refloated on 23 December.

A heavy gale on 28 July 1837 drove the *Britannia*, of Bideford, onto the rocks of Pwll Du Point where she became a wreck. Capt Bowden and his crew scrambled ashore.

The schooner *Diligence*, of St Ives, also got on the Lynch when bound from Hayle to Swansea with copper ore on the afternoon of 20 December 1837. George Holland the Lloyd's agent, Capt Evans of the *Penrice Castle*, his mate John Button, John Guy master of the *Susanna*, pilot William Lewis and two others manned a boat and brought the schooner's crew ashore. Though she was in an exposed position, the weather held enabling the cargo to be discharged and the vessel refloated.

Early on the morning of 30 January 1838 the brig *Hero*, of Montrose, Capt Allen, ran ashore at Port Eynon in poor visibility. She was nearing the end of a voyage from Chile to Swansea with a cargo of copper ore and Nicaragua wood. The vessel struck at low water, the crew got ashore, but she broke up when the flowing tide covered her.

At 5 p.m. on Saturday 24 March, a sloop was

seen in Rhosili Bay almost on her beam ends, her cargo having shifted in the heavy swell brought on by a strong south-west wind. Watchers saw the sails taken in and the vessel brought to an anchor as she righted. The crew was then seen to leave but, as they came ashore, the boat capsized a quarter of a mile from the beach drowning all three. The boat came in on the tide and identified the sloop as the *Eliza Jane*, of Dungarvan. A body recovered at Rhosili the next evening was identified as that of Philip Vincent the sloop's master. In his trouser pocket was a knife bearing his initials, and he was tattooed with the square and compasses and "other masonic symbols" and also wore a medallion of the Virgin. The 63 ton sloop *Jeremiah*, of Bideford, was wrecked near the Worm on the same day but her crew survived by scrambling ashore when she struck the rocks.

The schooner *Feronia*, Ulverston to Aberavon with iron ore, struck the Mixon on 24 July 1838. She got off on the flood but sank as she was being run for Mumbles. The crews of the Swansea pilot boats *Victoria* and *Sarah Jane* saved James Anthony and two crew from the water. As the pilots were bound down channel, the rescued were put aboard the schooner *Wave* and landed at Swansea. The Lifeboat Institution, at its meeting of 19 September, voted cash rewards to the rescuers and its silver medal to John Rees, master of the *Wave*, "in consideration of his kind and humane conduct to the rescued by taking them on board his vessel and administering such comforts and assistance as they required".

The *Sisters*, of St Ives, Binney master, was bound to Swansea when a south-west gale drove her ashore at Rhosili on the evening of 27 November 1838. The crew got ashore but the vessel broke up within a week.

The Chester sloop *Grace*, Owen master, with a cargo of oak from Bridgwater to Liverpool, was swamped by heavy seas and forced ashore at Rhosili at the beginning of February 1839. She became a wreck on the exposed beach and was sold by auction on the 22nd.

A heavy north-west gale with high seas caused casualties on the afternoon of Tuesday 21 January 1840. Lloyd's agent at Llanelli reported "A schooner has gone to pieces near Whitford. From a mark on a handspike she is supposed to be the *Dolphin*, of Dartmouth". At the inquest held on the body of a crew member, evidence was given by Rowland Taylor who was on the cliffs when he saw the distressed vessel. She was sailing close in shore and struck the beach near Burry Holms. The schooner capsized, drifted onto the rocks and quickly broke up. Taylor thought that she carried a crew of five. He saw one man climb the rigging and another scramble along a mast as it fell towards the shore. Taylor and his companions tried to reach him but a sea carried him to his death. The vessel was later positively identified by her boat which washed ashore. The gale also claimed the lives of the crew of the schooner *Shepherd*, of Liverpool, which was wrecked at Worms Head. The crew of the barque *Suir*, of Waterford, were lucky when she was driven onto the beach at Llanmadoc and held together. They had cut away the mainmast in an effort to save her. After two months of hard work the vessel was towed to Llanelli for repair.

In an attempt to improve safety in the approaches to the Burry estuary, Llanelli Harbour Trust moored a vessel in the south channel about one mile north of Burry Holms. She had the dual role of lightship and accommodation for the duty pilots,

The paddle-steamer *City of Bristol* was wrecked on Rhosili beach with the loss of twenty seven lives. Her engines are exposed at low water of spring tides. *(Author's photo)*

and was placed on station in March 1840 in lieu of the No 1 buoy in the Lynch pool.

Though it is now 150 years since she was lost, the remains of the *City of Bristol* may still be seen at low water of spring tides north of Diles Lake on Rhosili beach. This 210 ton wooden paddle steamer was launched at Hotwells, Bristol, in May 1827 and had a successful career on the routes from Bristol to Dublin, Cork and Waterford. The packet left

Waterford on the morning of Tuesday 17 November 1840 bound to Bristol with a crew of twenty two and seven passengers. As cargo, she carried fifteen bullocks below deck, two hundred and eighty pigs in pens on deck, 370 barrels of oats, 113 barrels of barley, two tierces of lard and 120 flitches of bacon. Soon after sailing it came on to blow so the commander, John Stacey, put back to Duncannon where they sheltered until 10.45 that evening. At 6 a.m. next day they were off the Smalls when it began to blow from south-east. Coming up channel, they saw St Govans Head at noon and made out Caldy light at about 4.45 on Wednesday afternoon. As it was still blowing hard, and visibility was poor with rain squalls, Capt Stacey told the men on deck that he would seek shelter to the north of Worms Head. Soon after 6 p.m. land was seen to larboard (as the port side was then called) and the vessel struck. The engines were put astern but the ship would not come off, and was soon broadside to the heavy surf which pounded the open beach. Crew and passengers came on deck when she struck, but the sea ran too high to consider using the boats. It was low water and the crew decided to stay aboard hoping that the vessel would hold together and float in as the tide made. The cook, James Cromwell, and stewardess, Sarah Jordan, were swept to their deaths in spite of having been lashed to the rail by the seamen. At high water (soon after midnight) the vessel broke into three sections. A group of ten people were instantly swept away. The master, mate William Moore, and seamen Joseph Nicholas, James Stacey and William Poole had taken refuge in the fore rigging. The mast fell as the vessel broke up hurling Poole amongst the floating wreckage. He broke three ribs but was able to drag himself onto a paddle box. A large sea washed him off and carried him towards the beach. Had not local people on the beach seen his exhausted condition and dashed into the surf he would have died. Poole thought that he was the sole survivor until he met Thomas Hamlier, ship's carpenter, at the King's Head, Llangennith, where they were cared for by landlord William Tucker. Hamlier, a powerfully built man, had lashed himself to the wheel and held on until the vessel broke up. He then jumped in and swam ashore. He was bruised but otherwise unhurt and able to walk to Llangennith. The remaining twenty seven crew and passengers died that awful night.

The Bristol owners were informed of the ship's loss by letters from Silvanus Padley, their Swansea agent, and George Holland, Lloyd's agent of Cwm Ivy. A director, George Lunell, left Bristol by the mail coach on Saturday morning and got to the scene before daylight on Sunday accompanied by Capt Edwards of the *Mountaineer* steamer. They found the vessel completely broken up with the upper part of the engines visible at low water, and fragments of the hull scattered about the beach. Some bodies had already been recovered and an inquest held at the King's Head. Capt Stacey's body was taken back to Bristol for burial at his home at Pill at the mouth of the Avon. A Mrs Urquart arrived later that week. She put herself through the harrowing experience of viewing the bodies recovered each day until she recognised that of her brother Donald Frazer, the chief engineer, which she took to Bristol for burial. The large sections of wreckage were sold by auction and the owners then allowed local people to take the fragments for their own use. Three bullocks and seventy five pigs had swum ashore, and were herded to George Holland's farm.

The schooner *Fanny*, on passage from Newport to Bideford, put back for Mumbles when she met bad weather on the morning of 26 January 1841, but struck the Mixon and was wrecked. John Channon, the master, and his crew of two were saved by the Swansea pilot boat *Susan* skippered by George Bidder. At its meeting of 7 April, the Lifeboat Institution voted ten shillings each to Bidder and his assistants Walker, Blackmore and Johnson.

Exactly a year later the Wexford smack *Dart* parted her cables in a westerly gale while anchored at Mumbles. She was driven over the Greengrounds and sank with all hands in the middle of Swansea Bay.

The smack *Gurnet* was a regular trader carrying oysters from Mumbles to Bristol. On 17 March 1842 she attempted to enter Swansea in boisterous conditions and was driven ashore near the piers where she capsized drowning her crew of two Mumbles men Clement and Jones. The smack *Industry*, also of Mumbles, worked in the limestone trade. On Thursday 19 May 1842 she was sailing from Limpert Bay, Aberthaw, bound for Aberavon when she was found to be taking in water fast. In running for Mumbles she went down two miles south-east of the lighthouse. A passing vessel picked up the master but his crewman was lost.

The smack *Ann & Elizabeth*, of Aberthaw, Bridgwater to Milford with bricks, stranded on the Lynch during a violent gale on 13 January 1843. Her crew got ashore and next day were very surprised to find the vessel in one piece. After a week's work by Mansfield, the Llanelli shipbuilder, she was refloated by the Llanmadoc master mariners Howells, Richards and Gray.

Two Mumbles women were widowed and their twelve children left fatherless, when the oyster skiff *Sarah & Rachel*, owned by Capt Phillips of the Ship and Castle public house, Mumbles, capsized while dredging in the Mixon Pool on the afternoon of 22 April. A group of skiffs were working when the coastguard, at the lookout on Mumbles Hill, saw one capsize unnoticed by the others. A Neath pilot boat lying at Mumbles was despatched, recovered the skiff, but found no survivors. David John, Tom Davies, Noah Jones and John Evans had drowned.

The brig *Liverpool Packet* was bound to Penzance with 180 tons of coal loaded at Newport, when she lost her rudder and became unmanageable. She was abandoned by her crew near Flat Holm, but sailed herself down channel and was wrecked in Rhosili Bay on 6 October 1843.

In the early hours of 9 January 1844 the Swansea barque *Dorothy Gales*, Capt Gardnor, owned by John Richardson, ran ashore west of Port Eynon in thick fog. She was bound home with 450 tons of Cuban copper ore and at first was believed to be beyond saving. However, when the crew reboarded her on the ebb to recover their belongings, she was found to be sound and was later refloated.

A south easterly storm caught dozens of vessels, anchored at Mumbles, on a lee shore on 17 March 1844. The *Superior*, of St Ives, parted her cables and sank a number of oyster skiffs as she drove through the moorings. The *Charles*, of Llanelli, and *Rebecca*, of Bridgwater, ended up rolling their bilges out on the stony shore, but Capt Bowden of the barque *Underley*, bound to Cuba, saved his vessel by slipping the cable and putting to sea with the pilot.

The sloop *Spreacombe*, of Bridgwater, was anchored in thick fog on the night of 16 April 1844. The master, Capt Cox, was unsure of his position but could hear a ground sea surging on the shore. His vessel dragged her anchor and was carried onto the rocks of Whiteshell Point to the east of Caswell Bay. Unable to get ashore, the master and four hands spent five hours in the rigging. The wreck was seen from the shore and news sent to Mumbles. Three brothers Jenkins put off in a small boat and saved the crew shortly before the mast came down.

AUGUST GALE

An unseasonably violent gale struck the peninsula on 2 August 1844. The wind was initially from the south-west but later blew from all quarters. The schooner *Margaret*, whose master Thomas was a Rhosili man, on passage from Rotterdam to Bristol with wine, oil cake, cheese and provisions, was driven ashore in Broughton Bay and went to pieces; her crew saved themselves. The *Mary*, a Bridgwater schooner, was lost nearby drowning a woman passenger. The schooner *Thetis*, of Llanelli, sank at her anchors in Oxwich Bay driving her crew into the rigging. At dawn they were seen by Capt Marshall of the *Affo*, of Bideford, which was also at anchor having lost her canvas. Marshall launched his boat, made fast to his vessel and veered down on the wreck. Taking the four from the rigging he got them safely back to his vessel. The smack *Triton*, of Plymouth, Par to Swansea with copper ore, drove ashore on Port Eynon Point; five of the crew were swept overboard and drowned, but Capt Wilcock climbed along the bowsprit the end of which rested on a rock. He reached this precarious perch from which he was eventually swept into the sea. Luckily the next wave swept him onto a sandy beach and he survived. The sloop *Julia*, of Chepstow, Bridgwater to Dublin with bark and hay, went ashore at Worms Head drowning one man, and the *Anne* sank at her anchors in Mumbles roads: numerous other vessels were damaged. In the three weeks following this gale, nine bodies were recovered and buried at Rhosili.

In a gale on the morning of Thursday 10 October 1844, the barque *Jane Boyd*, of Aberdeen, parted her cables at Mumbles and collided with the ship *Frances*, of Liverpool, Valparaiso to Swansea with copper ore. The *Frances* was holed and sank in fifteen feet off West Cross so that her decks were dry at low water. Her crew of twenty landed in the longboat below Singleton, and after much effort the vessel was raised and got into harbour on Christmas Eve.

In April 1845 Carmarthen Town Council, concerned at the number of wrecks in Carmarthen Bay, petitioned Trinity House for a lighthouse to be erected on Worms Head. The brethren replied that they were willing to erect such a light and, to maintain it, would levy one eighth of a penny per ton on vessels which crossed a line from Morte Point (on the Devon coast) to the Worm. However, instead of building a lighthouse, Trinity House moored a lightvessel off the western end of the Helwick sandbank. The ship was placed on station on 1 October 1846 and a bright revolving light shown each night. The lightship was maintained until replaced by a navigation buoy in 1989.

In the winter of 1846-47 the commissioners enquiring into the state of education in Wales were visiting Gower schools. On 22 February 1847, David Lewis the assistant commissioner, visited the schools at Oystermouth. He described the boys' school as "slovenly and unsystematic". "I found but a thin attendance" he reported "there had been a wreck in the neighbourhood the day before, and all the bigger boys were gone to look at it". Wreckage

NOTICE TO MARINERS.

LIGHT NEAR THE HELWICKS SAND,

Off the Worms Head, in the Bristol Channel.

Trinity House, London,
7th Oct. 1846.

A Floating Light Vessel having, in fulfilment of the intention expressed in the advertisement from this House, dated the 2nd ult. been placed at her intended station off the West End of the Helwicks Sand, on Thursday, the 1st inst., Notice thereof is hereby given; and that a bright Revolving Light was exhibited on board the same on the evening of the said day, and will be continued every Night from Sunset to Sunrise.

This Vessel is moored in 13 fathoms at Low Water Spring Tides, and in the position indicated by the following Marks and Compass Bearings, viz.:—

Oxwich Point just open of Porth Einon Point, bearing E. by S. ⅜ S.

Rossilly Parsonage House, just open of Worms Island E. by N. ¼ N.

Caldy Light House N.N.W. ¼ W.
Worms Head N.E. by E. ¾ E.

By Order,

J. HERBERT, *Secretary.*

A lightship marked the dangerous Helwick sand for over one hundred and forty years. *(Lloyd's List)*

had first been noticed along the coast from the Worm to Mumbles on Friday 19 February. Todd, Comptroller of Customs, and Holland, Lloyd's agent, were informed and by the time they arrived at Oxwich large quantities of wool were coming ashore with the wreckage. The ship's papers also came in on the tide and identified the wrecked vessel as the barque *Brechin Castle*, of Dundee, John Baxter master, Port Adelaide for Swansea with 520 tons of copper ore from the Burra Burra mines, and 120 bales of wool, total value in excess of £17,000. A bag of newspapers and the Australian mail also floated in. The mail was dried and forwarded to London. On Saturday evening the body of a seaman was found wearing a lifejacket and the next day that of a child was recovered.

On Monday 22nd almost half the hull of the barque was found floating near the Mixon. The Swansea pilots attempted to tow it in but it broke free and was washed up at Limeslade. The other section of the hull was found at Oxwich. The barque had carried a crew of fifteen, along with the Winterbottom and Fairbourne families as passengers; all were lost. It was generally believed that the barque had been wrecked on the Helwick and it was thought possible that the new lightship had contributed to the loss. As the *Brechin Castle* had left Britain in February 1846 her master would not have known of the lightship. The first light he would have expected to see after Lundy was that at Mumbles. If he failed to notice the distance run from Lundy was short, he may have turned to port believing that he was entering Swansea Bay and put his vessel right across the bank.

The brig *Circassian*, inward bound with Cuban copper ore, was anchored at Mumbles when a westerly gale turned into a "perfect hurricane" on the evening of 6 December 1847. The vessel parted her cables, drifted up the bay and drove ashore at Swansea where she was swept by huge seas. Conditions were too bad to think of rescue, but by 5 a.m. next day an improvement allowed a tug to get alongside and take off some of the crew. Later two men returned to the vessel and took off the master, mate and two seamen. In the darkness they failed to return to the tug and were believed lost. At dawn the boat was seen drifting out of the bay on the ebb tide. The men were saved by pilot John George who found them baling furiously with their boots.

The Mixon claimed another victim on the morning of Monday 6 March 1848. Though the wind was not very strong, the sea ran high on the bank. "The Cambrian" reported that it was "supposed that the crew perished in the darkness of night unseen by any human being". It was some days before the vessel was identified as the Waterford brigantine *Earl Gowrie* bound home with a cargo of coal.

The British Association for the Advancement of Science met at Swansea in August 1848. As part of the proceedings Lt. Carte R.N. demonstrated his line-throwing rockets. A schooner was anchored off the piers and a rocket used to fire a line into the rigging. Two men were then carried ashore in the breeches buoy. Rockets were far more effective than the Manby mortar and were soon in use by the Life-saving Apparatus companies.

The smack *Eagle*, Porthcawl for her home port of Aberystwyth, was lost on the Cherrystone at Mumbles while working her way out of the anchorage on 26 October 1848; her crew rowed ashore. A month later the London barque *Arietta* was sailing cautiously up the coast bound to Swansea with Cuban copper ore. The night was clear above but hazy at sea level and the land could not be seen. The Helwick light had been made out and, with the wind in the north, the master had kept the vessel close in. At midnight on 27 November she struck the outer edge of the Mixon. Hands were sent aloft to make more sail but she would not come off. At low water the crew abandoned, but as they did so a swell drove the boat against the vessel's side and John McDougal, second mate, was knocked overboard and drowned. The master and thirteen hands rowed to the Neath tug *Dragonfly* lying at anchor at Mumbles. The tug was unable to get near the barque and she went to pieces on the flood.

The Swansea barque *Pascoe Grenfell* and the schooner *Victoria*, of Looe, both outward bound, collided off Port Eynon on the night of 16 January 1849. The schooner sank and her crew were picked up and landed at Mumbles by a passing vessel. The barque lost her jib-boom but was able to proceed.

('The Cambrian', Swansea Museum)

The brig *Mary Jones*, of Pictou (Nova Scotia), was bound from Pugwash to Liverpool with a cargo of deals and battens. At 2.30 on the afternoon of Friday 14 December 1849 land was seen through the rain and the vessel stood inshore so that the position could be determined. A coaster was hailed and the information they were given led the master of the *Mary Jones* to understand that they were off Bardsey Island. Though there was some scepticism, this was accepted and course was shaped for Holyhead. At 7 p.m. they realised that the vessel was near the shore and attempted to wear ship. The manoeuvre failed and the brig drifted onto the rocks where it was swept by heavy seas. The crew took to the main rigging, but when the masts fell they were hurled into a tangle of wreckage on deck. It was now every man for himself and most were able to jump into the sea and swim ashore to seek shelter on the rocks. Seaman Thomas Pollard called out that he had broken his legs and was trapped in the wreckage. No one was able to go to his assistance. At low water, the survivors heard feeble cries from the wreck and some got back aboard to find the master, Mark Maddison, badly hurt and trapped in a tangle of spars and rigging. He was freed, lowered over the side, and with great difficulty carried to the cliff top. It was midnight before they were able to get assistance and were taken in by the Bevan family of Overton. Tom Pollard's body was found at Salthouse Mere a few days later. The *Mary Jones* was well out of her course and had been wrecked between Port Eynon and Paviland. George Holland arranged the sale of the vessel's cargo where it lay along the coast.

The *Mary*, of Bideford, with a cargo of iron, parted from her anchors in a severe storm on 5 February 1850 and sank on the Greengrounds. It was the third shipwreck that her master had experienced in nine years.

The Port Talbot pilot boat *Mary* was wrecked on the rock ledges on the western side of Mumbles Head directly below the lighthouse on Friday 21 June 1850. Pilot John Matthews and his crew saved themselves by clinging to the rocks until low water.

At seven o'clock on the evening of Wednesday 7 August 1850 the coastguard on Mumbles Hill saw a small vessel founder on the Mixon. At low water next day a boat went off to the wreck and recovered her topmast, mainboom and boat. She proved to be the Port Eynon owned *Hope* with a cargo of oats from Waterford. Her crew of William Richards master, John Richards and Abraham Ace were drowned. The Richards' family grave at Rhosili records that William's body was found near Nash Point and buried in that parish on 17 August.

Part of the hull and rigging of a schooner were washed up at Port Eynon in the first week of December 1850. By the time it was sold, a week later, it had been identified as belonging to the *Courageux*, of Nantes, believed to have been inward bound for Swansea in ballast. The vessel and its crew were thought to have been victims of the storm which struck the Bristol Channel on 24 November.

At Christmas 1851 Port Eynon was once again plunged into mourning when the skiff *Springflower* was overwhelmed by a sudden westerly gale as she left the Bantum oyster haul on the eastern end of the Helwick. John Chalk, John Jenkins, James Rees and John Jones were drowned.

Gower's first lifeboat had been stationed at Mumbles in 1835 but had almost certainly made no rescues while there. She had been moved to

Swansea harbour in 1841 but, with the lack of an experienced shore organisation, had again made no services. That the other end of Gower had a lifeboat in 1852 will come as a surprise to most. A branch of the Shipwrecked Fishermen and Mariners Benevolent Society had been formed at Llanelli in 1840. Its main function was to reimburse seamen for clothing and belongings lost through shipwreck and to support widows and orphans. The society also formed a lifeboat branch to supplement the work of the older organisation, the R.N.L.I. In March 1852 the society forwarded a Beeching lifeboat to Llanelli. It was kept on davits on the lightship moored in the Lynch Pool one mile north of Burry Holms in a good position to deal with incidents in the Whitford area. The arrangement was unsatisfactory however, as the pilots who formed the crew would have been otherwise engaged during bad weather. All the society's boats were handed to the R.N.L.I. in 1854. The lifeboat was launched on 8 November 1855 to the ship *Elizabeth* seen in difficulties near Burry Holms, but the vessel got away without assistance. This lifeboat, named *Rescue*, remained at the station until it was closed in 1863, a new station having been opened at Pembrey on the other side of the Burry Estuary.

At dawn on Monday 6 December 1852 another wreck was seen on the Mixon. It was the *Pretty Maggy*, of Cork, Ballinacura to Cardiff in ballast. The crew of five and a passenger were lost. Most of the wreck floated ashore at Bracelet and was sold by auction at the Ship and Castle public house, Mumbles.

The 80 ton Milford smack *Ellen*, with a cargo of oats and butter for Bristol, was found to be leaking as she crossed Port Eynon Bay on 15 January 1853. The mate asked Peter Perkins, the skipper, to put her ashore at Slade but Perkins wanted to get her to Oxwich. The vessel, however, foundered off Oxwich Point drowning Perkins, who had gone below to get clothes. The third hand too went down with the vessel. The mate jumped overboard and began to swim ashore. On looking back, he saw the masthead above water and swam back to it. A boat went off from Port Eynon to take him ashore. Perkins' grave may still be seen at Oxwich Church.

When the Brazilian brig *Nettuno*, Swansea to Cape Verde Island with coal, struck the Greengrounds on 6 July 1853 she took in water fast and foundered south-east of Mumbles lighthouse. Constituting a hazard to shipping, her position was marked by a green wreck buoy. Two weeks later the Swansea pilot boat *Sarah Jane* was wrecked near Pwll Du. Her crew scrambled ashore.

In June the following year the brig *Irma*, of Bayonne, with coal from Cardiff, drove ashore near Worms Head and became a complete wreck.

The barque *Henrietta*, John Egan master, Cuba to Swansea with copper ore, stranded on the Mixon on the morning of 10 March 1855. She made distress signals but the boisterous conditions prevented pilots boarding and her crew abandoned. The next day conditions were better and a combined effort between the revenue cutter *Adder* and three pilots refloated the vessel and got her to port. The *Adder's* men were awarded £765 and the pilots £170.

The Sunderland brig *Anna Catherine*, bound to London with 350 tons of Powell's Dyffryn steam coal, was sheltering at Mumbles from a W.S.W. gale on the evening of 25 October 1855. The gale increased to hurricane force accompanied by torrential rain. The vessel parted her cables at 10 p.m. and drifted onto the Greengrounds where she unshipped her rudder and started the whole of her stern timbers. On the flood she rode over the banks and foundered at 2 a.m. next day. Capt Anderson and his crew took to the rigging from which they were rescued at daybreak by the crew of the tug *Beaufort*. The tug skipper, Griffith Rosser, was awarded a sovereign and the thanks of the R.N.L.I. inscribed on vellum. His crew were given ten shillings each.

One of Swansea's famous copper barques came to grief at Lucas Cove just west of Oxwich Point on the morning of 8 February 1856. The *Catherine Jenkins* was homeward bound having sailed from Santiago, Cuba, on 24 December 1855. At 4 p.m. on Thursday 7 February she was six miles north of Lundy. The weather was stormy and thick with drizzle. The course was east which was designed to take them to the approaches to Swansea Bay but at about 4 a.m. on the 8th the vessel struck. The look-outs had no indication of land until they heard the breakers. The barque immediately began to break up and the crew of eleven (five others had died of yellow fever at Santiago) took to the gig having found the longboat too heavy to manage. They had gone a few ship's lengths towards the shore when the boat capsized throwing all into the water. Only three men got to the rocks. They were the Portuguese cook Jeremiah Frightus, Tom Hughes the mate (a native of Carmarthen), and David Thompson 2nd mate. The cook then spotted able seaman Tom Harris struggling against the ground sea and bravely entered the water again to haul him ashore. The other seven were drowned. They were Capt Matthew Hodge, W.H. Reed the steward, John Payne apprentice, John Morse the carpenter, Michael Moore A.B., and Benjamin Austin and Richard Edwards ordinary seamen. Morse, Austin and Payne were all Swansea men, Austin being a member of a family prominent as sea pilots.

Tom Hughes remained on the shore for some hours and at 9 a.m. watched as the barque's masts fell and wreckage came ashore. Over the following weeks much of the cargo was recovered and taken to Swansea for the Cobre Mining Company. The remains of the hull were sold where they lay on the shore on 27 February and the masts, yards, anchors, cables and other materials came under the hammer at Swansea a month later. Charles Collins, the coroner, held the inquest on the body of John Morse at the King's Arms, High Street, Swansea, on Monday 11 February. The verdict was "Drowned from the swamping of the boat, by endeavouring to escape from the *Catherine Jenkins* which had stranded near Oxwich Point".

WRECK.---UNRESERVED SALE.

TO SHIP AND HOUSE BUILDERS.

Mr. THOS. GLOVER
Has been instructed

TO SELL BY AUCTION,

On WEDNESDAY, FEBRUARY 27, 1856.

THE First Portion of the WRECK of the "CATHERINE JENKINS," where it now lies, at OXWICH POINT, GOWER, which consists of her Two Sides and part of her Bottom, which are copper fastened; with her broken spars and several smaller, lots, adapted for farm or building purposes. Also, a BOAT.

The Sale will take place at Eleven o'clock for Twelve precisely, forenoon.

Five members of the crew of the *Catherine Jenkins* died of yellow fever as they loaded copper ore in Cuba. The master and six others were drowned when the barque was wrecked on Oxwich Point on the return trip. ('*Swansea Journal*', Swansea Museum)

TUG TO THE RESCUE

In the first week of September 1856, the Trinity House steamer *Vestal* replaced the buoy marking the Mixon shoal with a bell buoy. The Mixon bell is still a welcome sound at Mumbles and is regarded as a sign of good weather to come (the breeze has to be from south for the bell to be heard on shore).

"There is no roadstead in the Bristol Channel which is more securely protected from the dangers consequent upon violent gales of wind, or more easily accessible than that of the Mumbles" trumpeted "The Cambrian", but on the night of 27 September 1856, a S.W. gale backed to S.E. and increased to storm force. The vessels at anchor were now exposed to the full fury of the wind and to the short steep sea which builds up when the wind is in that quarter. Eight vessels sank at their anchors, nine parted their cables and were stranded on the shore and a further five were damaged. The coastguard galley manned by Chief Officer Dillon, William Evans boatswain, William Griffiths and James Sullivan, saved the crews of the schooners *Monkey*, of Drogheda, and *Western Star*, of New Ross, while a shore boat manned by brothers Jenkin and William Jenkins, and Tom Michael, saved the crews of the *Emmet*, of Aberaeron, the brigantine *Pioneer*, of Exeter, and the *Happy Return*, of Padstow. The schooner *Wave* also sank but her crew rowed themselves ashore. Among the vessels driven ashore were the schooner *Swiftsure*, of Gloucester, and the barque *Pascoe Grenfell* waiting for a berth at the copper ore wharves at Swansea. At dawn the shore was strewn with wreckage, casks and seamen's chests: "ships sunk, ships ashore, ships damaged met the eye to whichever quarter it turned".

The lugger *Juanita*, bound from Swansea to Seville, was sheltering from a gale when she sank at her anchors at Mumbles on 15 March 1857. The vessel's hull and masts were salvaged and put up for sale at Swansea four months later.

The smack *Louis*, Llanelli to Rouen with coal, lost her mainsail in a squall on 2 January 1858 and was driven up channel. Her crew of three men and two boys, one of whom had suffered a broken leg, abandoned and were picked up by the Tenby fishing smack *Ann*. The *Louis* drifted ashore and was wrecked on Port Eynon Point.

In spite of its bell buoy the Mixon continued to be a hazard: on 11 June 1858 the *Busy*, of Beaumaris, Barrow to Neath with iron ore, struck the bank and sank as she was being run for the shore.

A gale on 2 October overwhelmed the *Hazard*, of Westport (County Mayo), which went down off Oxwich. Her crew of four were picked up from their boat. On the same day the *Emily*, of Bridgwater, was driven ashore and wrecked at Port Eynon with only one survivor.

The vulnerability of Mumbles roads to easterly gales was again demonstrated on 19 October 1858. A north-east gale blew throughout the day driving a schooner onto the Middle Head. At 10 a.m. the pilot boat *Neptune* lost her cables and was driven onto the beach where her bottom timbers and deck gave way. Five hours later at high water the pilot boat

Sarah also drove ashore. She went in high up the beach and was scuttled by her crew to reduce damage. Five of the locally owned oyster skiffs also parted their moorings and were wrecked on the beach.

When the South Dock was opened at Swansea in September 1859, the Harbour Trust lifeboat took part in the ceremony. Though the lifeboat had been placed at Mumbles in 1835 and moved to Swansea in 1841, it did not perform its first service until May 1860 when the crew was saved from the brig *Success*, of South Shields, wrecked on Neath bar.

The 95 ton ketch *Friends* foundered on the Helwick, with the loss of her crew of six, on 28 September 1859.

The storm which raged over much of western Britain on 25 October 1859 was described by Rear-Admiral Robert Fitzroy F.R.S. as a "complete horizontal cyclone". Today it is still known as the *"Royal Charter* gale" after the steamship wrecked at Moelfre, Anglesey, with the loss of over four hundred lives. Gower escaped lightly; four vessels drove ashore at Mumbles, but only one, the smack *Eliza* of Llanelli, became a wreck, and the sloop *Union*, John Gardner master, Bridgwater to Llanelli with railway sleepers, was driven ashore without loss of life at Worms Head. The weather remained stormy for more than a week and on 31 October the schooner *Robert Henry*, of Hayle, foundered four miles off Pennard when bound to Swansea; her crew rowed ashore. Sir Gardner Wilkinson was at Rhosili at the time of this storm, staying with his brother-in-law the rector and had witnessed the wreck of the *Union*. On 7 November Wilkinson wrote to the R.N.L.I. asking for a Manby's apparatus to be sent to the village for use at a wreck. He told the Institution that the rector was prepared to "keep it in the church and very willing to take charge of it"

and added "there are men in the village sufficiently intelligent to learn all that is necessary respecting its working". It would be another twenty years before the Board of Trade formed a life-saving apparatus company (rocket crew) at Rhosili.

The brigantine *William & Mary*, bound from Swansea to her home port of Youghal, was caught in a squall on 28 December 1859 and drove onto Mumbles Head at 7 a.m. The vessel broke up losing her cargo of coal but her crew survived.

On 1 January 1861 the Austrian brig *Andrina*, Capt Remuda, fell in with the brig *Camille*, of la Rochelle, flying distress signals about three miles south of the Helwick. The Austrians lowered a boat and with some difficulty, due to a nasty cross sea, saved the crew of six who were exhausted from pumping their sinking vessel.

On 11 March the crew of the Helwick lightship saw four vessels scudding before a heavy gale. Three of them sailed past the lightship but the fourth drifted by bottom-up with a tangle of spars and rigging alongside. The lightship crew were powerless to assist. A couple of days later the masts and rigging of a vessel were recovered and towed to Milford where they were identified as coming from the Austrian ship *Zoe* which had left Cardiff for Venice some weeks earlier.

Late on the evening of 2 September 1861 the pilot boat *Rival*, anchored at Mumbles, got under way when signals were seen through the sound. Thinking that a vessel was signalling for a pilot, they ran out to the outer roads but found nothing and were returning when a voice was heard calling from the water. They tacked towards the voice and found a man clinging to a capsized boat. He was Francis Matcovich who had been at the wheel of the brigantine *Villiers*, which had struck the Mixon at about 10.30 p.m. The 142 ton vessel, carrying coal from Cardiff to Alicante, had been south of Worms Head when the S.W. wind freshened forcing Capt James Pill to put about for Mumbles. The *Rival's* men continued to search and shortly heard another man calling. They found the cook, Joseph Rogers, supporting himself on two oars and got him aboard. Two others who had been in the boat were lost. The rescued said that four others were still aboard the wreck.

Seeing the seas that were breaking on the Mixon, pilot Tom Davies returned to the roads and told the skipper of the tug *Talbot*. David Tanner, master of the *Talbot*, was later to say that the *Rival's* men did not tell him that there were men still on the wreck. As a result it was 4 a.m. next day before they weighed to go to the Mixon. It was then that they saw men in the rigging. Having no boat on the tug and not wishing to risk his vessel near the bank, Tanner was returning to the anchorage to borrow a boat when he met the tug *Beaufort*, Capt Philip Deusbury. The *Beaufort* immediately went to the wreck and found one man on the tops'lyard and three in the rigging. Deusbury took the tug in close and lines were thrown to the men "But" he reported "they were too timid, and did not like to venture". Deusbury then backed the tug between the masts of the sunken vessel and saved the four: Capt James Pill, Robert Murphy mate, and boys George Nance (nephew of the owner) and William Weston.

At the Board of Trade inquiry which began on 4 September, Capt Pill admitted he was "a little out in his reckoning in coming up the coast", and did not see the Mumbles light until after the vessel had struck. He suggested that the light should be sectored to show a red light in the direction of the Mixon. Capt Elliott, Inspecting Commander of the Coastguard, who conducted the inquiry, thought that a lightvessel placed to mark the Scarweather Sands would be most useful to vessels running up channel. (The Scarweather lightship was placed on station, about eight miles south of Mumbles Head, in 1862 and remained in use until 1989.) The details of the *Villiers* rescue were reported to the Board of Trade who sent a draft to Capt Elliott with instructions to award £3 to Capt Deusbury, £1 each to his crew and ten shillings to the tug's boy. The R.N.L.I. also made a monetary award.

In February 1862 a mast was erected at the coastguard station on Mumbles Hill so that storm signals could be hoisted to warn passing shipping.

At 1.30 on the afternoon of Wednesday 5 March 1862, Thomas Powell of Newton was in Langland Bay when he saw a schooner founder a mile or so west of Mumbles Head. He alerted the coastguard who launched their galley. It was joined by the pilot boats *Vivian*, of Swansea, and *Kate*, of Port Talbot. When they reached the scene the mastheads were visible but no survivors were found. The vessel's boat was recovered and served to identify her as the *Victoria & Albert*, of Dungarvan, which had been bound to Swansea with copper ore.

The barque *Laconic* sailed from Swansea on 18 February 1863 with coal for Tenerife. The next day in a dead calm with thick fog she drifted onto the western end of the Helwick and was abandoned as she broke up. Her crew got to Rhosili in the boats.

On 8 October 1863 the brig *J.O.*, of Sunderland, was being towed out of the Burry estuary laden with 475 tons of culm when the tow parted as she met a vicious groundsea outside Whitford Point. The crew escaped when the brig drove ashore and was wrecked.

George Holland, Lloyd's agent for the coast from

Pennard Pill to Whitford Point, had died aged eighty six in April 1862. His successor, George Gibbs of Port Eynon, was not appointed until January 1864, but within a couple of weeks had his first casualty almost on his doorstep. George's mother Harriet kept a notebook which survives to this day. Under 10 February 1864 she recorded: "a brigantine got ashore by Skysea and became a total wreck. She was from Plymouth with limestone ballast. Five of the crew lodged at J.Bevan's till Friday 12th". The vessel was the *Peri*, of Port Talbot, which twice missed stays and ran head-on onto the rocks in a heavy sea at 4 a.m. The crew got onto the rocks and when they were seen at dawn, a boat went off and brought them ashore. The vessel went to pieces and the men lost their clothing and belongings. George Gibbs had the task of selling the wreck, but a letter to "The Cambrian" accused him of keeping the more valuable cables and anchors for a less than public auction between his friends at the Ship Inn.

George Gibbs was again busy when the brig *Industrious*, Llanelli to Malta with coal, went ashore on the sand at Nackershole, Port Eynon, on the morning of 19 September 1864. Being an old vessel she quickly broke up but much of her cargo was saved.

A heavy S.W. gale on Friday 18 November 1864 caused the loss of three vessels. The smack *Desirée*, of St Vaast, Swansea to le Havre with coal, ran back before the storm and anchored in Oxwich Bay at 4 a.m. At eight she parted her cables and drove ashore. John Clement of Penmaen, and brothers John and William Bevan of Nicholaston, saw the vessel and ran to the beach. They arrived just as the crew of five were coming ashore. The boat capsized in the surf and three men got ashore leaving Capt Thomes and the boy exhausted in the break-

ers. The three local men dashed in and dragged them to safety. The five Frenchmen were taken to Clement's house where the master and boy were put to bed to recover. John Clement and the Bevan brothers were presented with the bronze medal of the Royal Humane Society during a service at Penmaen Church by the rector, Rev Edward James, on 16 April 1865. A year later the three received silver medals from the French government.

The second vessel lost that day was the schooner *Hectorine*, of Conway. On passage from Cork to Llanelli, she was riding at anchor inside Worms Head when she parted and drove up the bay towards Llangennith. The crew got ashore when the vessel broke up. A few days later wreckage, including the stern board of the *Lady of the Lake*, of Bristol, was found at Caswell. More wreckage washed up at Oxwich and the vessel's boat was picked up off shore. Two weeks after the storm, a letter was received by Mumbles coastguard from Braunton, N. Devon, making enquiries of the vessel, her master Capt Reed and crew.

On the morning of 26 January 1865 a derelict schooner was found ashore at Overton. George Gibbs arrived to find the *Francis & Ann*, of Jersey, already breaking up and scattering her cargo of oranges along the tide line. Working against time, Gibbs landed the schooner's materials and what remained of her cargo. Later that day when informing Lloyd's of the wreck he reported that there was no sign of the vessel's boat or crew. A day later news came from Milford that Capt Vibert and his crew had been landed there. The *Francis & Ann*, which had left Palermo on 22 December bound for Bristol, had struck the Helwick during a snowstorm. Her crew had escaped in the boat and found refuge on the lightship before being taken to Milford by a passing steamer. The oranges were sold by auctioneer D. Edwards after George Gibbs had travelled Gower advertising the sale with handbills.

The day after the wreck of the "orange vessel", a wreck was found on the beach at Langland. She was the Cardiff pilot cutter No 20, *Robin Hood*, which had got under the bows of a barque off Ilfracombe and been run down. Her crew had survived.

The ever vigilant crew of the Swansea pilot boat *Grenfell* were at hand when a pleasure boat carrying a party off Neath businessmen and their guests capsized in the race off Mumbles Head on 23 August. They saved five but three others were drowned.

The smack *Emmanuel Adrien*, with a cargo of potatoes, stranded at Llanmadoc on 22 November 1865 and became a total loss.

The *Eliza Jane* sailed from Cardiff on Tuesday 20 March 1866. At seven that evening she was abandoned in a sinking condition and foundered off Worms Head. The crew of six were picked up by the schooner *Equity*, of New Quay, and landed at Swansea.

Three days later a heavy sou'west gale struck the coast. The schooner *Electric Flash*, of Hayle, with 100 tons of coal from Porthcawl, drove ashore at Port Eynon and became a total loss. The crew were saved by a boat from the shore, and sixty tons of the cargo were sold to the village, the rest being taken to Mumbles. On the same day the lifeboat *Martha & Anne*, which had been stationed at Mumbles since January that year, launched to the brig *Vesta*, of Whitby, which had been driven from the anchorage and foundered on the inner Greengrounds. Coxswain Jenkins took the lifeboat over the deck of the wreck to snatch the crew of seven from the fore-rigging.

Two days after leaving Swansea with coal for Barcelona, the brig *Chasseur*, of Nantes, put back in the face of bad weather to shelter off Mumbles. On the evening of 10 September 1866 she parted in a strong gale and went down near the Greengrounds. The incident went unseen from the shore and the crew spent an uncomfortable four hours in the rigging before rescue by Capt John Withers and the crew of the tug *Tweed*. Capt Withers was awarded a presentation telescope by the French government.

Two days of severe westerly gales produced many casualties in January 1867. On the 7th the Pembrey lifeboat *City of Bath* rescued eight from the brigantine *Seraphim*, of Dunkirk, wrecked towards Kidwelly. On the next morning with the gale unabated a lugger was seen beating over the middle spit of the Lynch sand off Whitford. The *City of Bath* launched and threaded her way through the maze of channels of Burry bar. As they approached, the crew could be seen in the rigging with the seas making a clean breach over them. Running alongside, the Pembrey men got the crew of six safely aboard. The vessel, the *Espoir*, of Nantes, with coal from Swansea, broke up and washed ashore at Llanmadoc. Soon after landing the Frenchmen, the Pembrey crew were told that a brig could be seen riding at anchor near Burry Holms in a distressed state. The *City of Bath* was again launched but when she got alongside the vessel, the *Zenith*, of Sunderland, the crew found her almost submerged and abandoned. The lifeboat returned to her station through heavy following seas which filled her to the gunwhales on two occasions. Later that day the *Zenith's* boat, and the bodies of her crew were found on the beach at Broughton.

Just a month later the Prussian brig *Fortuna*, Capt Breckwoldt, with cotton and sugar from Puerto Cabelo (Venezuela) for Liverpool, was caught in a storm and struck by a succession of seas which swept her decks and brought down her masts. She was driven before the storm and run ashore in Broughton Bay driving well up the beach on a full tide. Much of her cargo was salvaged, and though she became a wreck, her sails and materials were recovered and sold by auctioneer Edward Howard at Swansea.

A vessel long remembered in Gower as the "Annie Monie" was wrecked at Port Eynon on 10 March 1867. She was the Whitstable brig *Anemone*, Newhaven to Cardiff in ballast, which went ashore at night during a stiff east wind with snow squalls.

WRECK SALE.

Mr. E. HOWARD,

WILL SELL BY AUCTION

At the hour of Three o'clock in the Afternoon, On Friday, the 8th of March, 1867, opposite the Custom House, Swansea,

THE whole of the SAILS, lately belonging to the Prussian Brig "Fortuna," wrecked at Llanmadock, Gower, and removed to Swansea for the convenience of sale, consisting of 2 Mainsails, 2 Boom Foresails, 2 Foresails, 2 Topsails, 2 Gallant Sails, 1 Topgallant Sail, 1 Topmast Staysail, 1 Gaff Topsail, 1 Main Trysail, 3 Jibs, 2 Staysails, 1 Fore Staysail, 6 Stunsails, 2 Boat Sails, 4 Awnings, Colours, Signals, Flags, Charts, and sundries

The Sails are all in good order and part of them nearly new, and will be sold without reserve.

For further particulars apply to the Auctioneer, 8 Somerset Place, Swansea, or to Mr. G. A. Bevan, Prussian Vice Consul, Swansea.

Bound from Venezuela to Liverpool, the brig *Fortuna* was disabled by a storm and driven up channel to be wrecked at Llanmadoc. Her cargo of cotton and sugar was recovered in a damaged state. *('The Cambrian', Swansea Museum)*

George Gibbs arranged accommodation for the master, crew of seven and the pilot, who stayed in the village for four days until arrangements for the sale of the wreck were complete. On the 14th they left for Swansea in Grove's horsebus.

Soon after dawn on Monday 13 January 1868, Charles Ridell of Llanelli Customs saw a vessel stranded on the north ridge off Whitford Point. Boarding the vessel, the Cardiff brig *Albion*, with a cargo of copper ore and esparto grass from Almeria, he found the galley fire still alight and a cat aboard, but no sign of the crew. Later that day Richard Thomas found the bodies of the brig's mate, John Nicholls, and able seaman Carl Zaschob, on Whitford beach. The next day farmer George Edwards found five more bodies on Llanrhidian marsh. The crew had evidently drowned while attempting to get ashore. An inquest was held at Cheriton by Edward Strick, district coroner. Benjamin Thomas, tallow chandler of Newport, identified one body as that of his son William a sixteen year old ordinary seaman. The wife of David Williams, the *Albion*'s master, had come down from Cardiff to view the bodies. Her husband's was not amongst them but she was able to identify those of the mate and cook.

THE MOST DISTRESSING WRECK

Harriet Gibbs noted in her diary on 23 January 1868 that her son George, Lloyd's agent: "was sent for to Rosilly at 2 o'clock in the morning, a vessel ashore and all perished. It was an awful gale and sea running mountains. There was a heart rending scene to look at. Eleven vessels all to pieces, having come out of Llanelly in the evening and the wind died away, the sea made and they all got ashore on Rosilly sand and Llangenny, Brufton and the banks. The shore was all strewed with the wrecks. Fifteen vessels came out and eleven can be seen the remains; the others are supposed to be gone, and the crews of them, as they could, left the vessels and some of them got to the hulk. How many poor fellows is gone, the account is not known. This is the most distressing wreck that was ever heard of on this coast".

Bad weather had prevented vessels sailing from Llanelli for some days, but on the afternoon of Wednesday 22 January there was a light northerly breeze and a fleet of nineteen colliers left. Most sailed independently but a string of five was towed down the estuary by the tug *Royal Princess*. As they rounded Whitford Point they could see that though the wind was light there was a terrific groundsea on the bar. As they crossed the bar in the vicinity of the hulk lightship, the breeze died away. A few vessels that were already clear were able to get sea room and arrived safely at their destinations, but others were now at the mercy of the sea and were driven ashore at Rhosili, Broughton and Llangennith.

John Parrot, a pilot of thirteen years experience at Llanelli, was aboard the schooner *Mary Fanny*, of Amlwch, as she was towed out by the tug. The tow parted as they passed Whitford lighthouse. Sail was made and the vessel was going down the south channel "with a nice little breeze" and steering towards the pilot hulk *Ceres*. Abreast the No 2 buoy, the schooner was struck by a sea which so frightened a young boy in the crew that he too jumped into the boat as Parrot left to board the *Ceres*. The boy was very fortunate for the *Mary Fanny* was wrecked in Rhosili Bay with the loss of five lives.

Joshua Boom of Appledore was a member of the crew of the polacca schooner *Ann*, of Bideford, which was struck by a huge sea near the lighthouse and lost her mainmast. The vessel became unmanageable and drifted ashore in Broughton Bay at about 8 p.m. The crew had abandoned and got aboard the lightship. The crews of five other vessels also abandoned and found refuge there. At dawn there was a scene of devastation: the *Mary Fanny*, *Water Lily*, the *Onward* of Llanelli, *Jeune Celine* of Jersey, *Huntress* of Workington, and *Amethyst* of Dublin, were all ashore having lost some or all of their men. The *Brothers* of Llanelli, and the brigantine *Roscius* were also ashore though their crews had survived.

Other vessels too were thought to have been lost, but on Thursday afternoon the Barnstaple smack *Elizabeth & Ann* put into Tenby in a disabled state. The crew had taken eleven hours to pump the six feet of water from her hold, the master had twice been washed overboard but survived, and the vessel had lost her boat, water cask and binnacle. The following Monday news came that the *Eliza*, of Jersey, which was also feared lost, had got away and reached St Malo with her cargo. Though the death toll was at first believed to be about fifty it was reduced to eighteen after careful enquiry.

The inquest into the deaths was opened on Friday 24 January at the Farmers Arms, Llanmadoc, by Edward Strick. The rector, Rev J.D. Davies, was foreman and most of the jurymen farmers of the district. Five bodies had then been recovered. After evidence of identification had been heard the proceedings were adjourned for three days. When it resumed a further nine bodies had been found. As the jury returned its verdict of "found drowned" a fifteenth body was recovered.

The jury recommended that a lifeboat be once again stationed on the hulk lightship and that a

---

LLANELLY, CARMARTHENSHIRE.

To be Sold by Public Auction,

At the CARMARTHENSHIRE DOCK,

By Messrs. THOMAS HAND & CO.,

On TUESDAY, March 10th, 1868,

THE HULL and MATERIALS of the Brigantine "BROTHERS," of Llanelly, 132 Tons Register, and Burthen about 220 Tons. Also, the MATERIALS of the wrecked Brigantine, "ROSCIUS," and the Schooner "WATER LILY," of Llanelly, consisting of SAILS, ROPES, CABLES, ANCHORS, and BOATS. Sale to commence at 12 o'clock precisely.

The *Brothers*, *Roscius* and *Water Lily* were among a dozen vessels wrecked at Llanmadoc on the evening of 22 January 1868. Eighteen seamen lost their lives. (*'The Cambrian'*, Swansea Museum)

mast be erected on Cwm Ivy Tor so that the state of the sea on the bar could be signalled to Llanelli. The R.N.L.I. quickly responded to the request for a boat and, at its meeting of 6 February, ordered one to be built. The boat, named *James & Elizabeth* was the gift of Miss Anne White of Plymouth, and was built of iron by Hamilton of Liverpool. She was 26ft long with a crew of six pulling five oars. She arrived in April 1869 and was once again kept on the lightship. The arrangement however proved to be unworkable and the station was closed when a larger lifeboat was placed at Pembrey in October 1871.

The schooner *Corliana*, Clonakilty to Newport in ballast, was driven ashore at Llanmadoc by a strong S.W. gale on the evening of 13 December 1869 and became a complete wreck; her crew got ashore.

During a heavy gale on Thursday 31 December 1869 the brig *Nuavo Plauto*, of Trieste, bound to Neath with grain from the Black Sea, parted her cables at Mumbles and foundered on the Greengrounds; her crew rowed ashore. On the same day the barque *Artistic*, of and from Newport to Brazil with coal, stranded on the Helwick. The whole crew except for the master and two men abandoned and got ashore in the boats. The vessel refloated on the flood and was got to Swansea with the assistance of two pilot boats. Two days later a small boat was found adrift in Swansea Bay. It contained the body of William John Brown a seaman of the *Eliza*, of Plymouth, a regular Swansea trader. There was no sign of the vessel or of the rest of the crew, but ten days later the vessel's sternboard was found on the rocks west of Langland.

Soon after dawn on Thursday 23 June 1870 the steamer *Sheldrake*, of Liverpool, bound from

Swansea to Bordeaux, collided with the 96 ton schooner *Mary*, of Portmadoc, about four miles south-west of Oxwich Point. The schooner, Barrow to Cardiff with pig iron, sank rapidly drowning the wife of John Roberts, the master. One of the steamer's men was killed by a falling spar. The *Mary*'s survivors got aboard the *Sheldrake* which returned to Swansea for repairs.

A westerly storm caused many shipping casualties on the Cornish and Welsh coasts on 12 October 1870. The schooner *Joseph et Marie*, bound from Carloforte (Sardinia) with a cargo of zinc ore, foundered in the entrance channel at Swansea, while in the crowded anchorage at Mumbles the schooner *Brigand*, of Faversham, was sunk in a collision. Both crews survived, in the latter case the tug *Pero Gomez* was quickly on the scene to pluck the crew from the water.

Larger square-rigged vessels undertook foreign voyages, but rarely made coastal passages. If they discharged at one British port and needed to load at another, they were usually towed around the coast by a steam tug. This required a smaller crew, and the quantity of ballast required for towing was less than that for sailing. It was this smaller ballast and a sudden gale which caused the loss of the barque *Daring* on 9 March 1871. She left Swansea at high water (about 8 a.m.) that day in tow of the tug *Cambria*, Stephen Hazell master. The barque was to load at Cardiff and carried a crew of six being the master, two mates, an apprentice and two riggers. The tug towed the vessel out to pass west of the Scarweather but a westerly gale came up. They were about four miles off shore south of Caswell when it was decided to put back for Swansea Bay. The tug failed to tow the barque around and the tow was slipped to allow her to make sail in an attempt

to wear ship. All the while the barque was drifting down the coast on the ebb and shorewards with the wind. An attempt at reconnecting the tow failed. The tug master now realised that the vessel would go ashore and attempted to save the crew, but as he went alongside they abandoned from the other side to row into Hunt's Bay. The tug crew saw the boat capsize leaving only two swimming. They got hold of one but lost their grip. All six of the *Daring's* crew were drowned and the vessel went ashore and was wrecked at Pwll Du.

At ten o'clock on the morning of Friday 21 April 1871, the Neath pilot boat *Black Swan*, Jeremiah Gilbert pilot, was returning to Mumbles after attending inward bound vessels. Off the head she sailed through wreckage amongst which was a waterlogged boat with two bodies across the gunwhales. The bodies were recovered and a note made of the name Samuel Dunstone painted on the boat's transom. At nine the previous evening the schooner *Cornish Diamond*, of Truro, bound from Newport to Plymouth, of which Dunstone was master, had been spoken by another pilot boat as she made her way towards Mumbles. It was surmised that the vessel had been yet another victim of the Mixon. Later in the day part of the deck, stern and figurehead came ashore in Bracelet Bay.

At the inquest, James Dunstone of Port Lowe near Truro, identified one of the bodies as that of his brother Samuel, aged forty five, who lived at Plymouth. The stone which once marked Dunstone's grave now forms part of the path at the rear of Oystermouth Church. Its inscription "He leaves behind him an affectionate wife and two dear children to mourn his loss" is, sadly, being steadily worn away.

Two hours before high water on the morning of

In Affectionate Remembrance of SAMUEL MORSE DUNSTONE OF FEOCK Cornwall MASTER MARINER AGED 33 YEARS WHO WAS DROWNED ON THE NIGHT OF APRIL 20TH 1871 BY HIS SHIP THE CORNISH DIAMOND OF Truro STRIKING ON THE MIXON SANDS AND BECOMING A TOTAL WRECK WHEN ALL HANDS PERISHED, HE LEAVES BEHIND HIM AN AFFECTIONATE WIFE AND TWO DEAR CHILDREN TO MOURN HIS LOSS

This gravestone may be seen in the churchyard of All Saints, Oystermouth. *(Author's photo)*

Thursday 11 January 1872, the 300 ton steamship *Hazard*, of Leith, was running at full speed on passage from Rouen to Swansea in ballast when she struck the rocks at Port Eynon. She carried a crew of sixteen one of whom was injured as she struck. The steamer filled and sank within a few minutes and became a total loss. The wrong course was being steered and Capt Campbell had his certificate suspended for three months. The Board of Trade inquiry also censured the mate, who had charge at the time of the loss, for not informing the master of the decreased visibility.

On 30 October 1872 the Pembrey lifeboat, *Stanton Meyrick of Pimlico*, threaded her way through the maze of channels to reach the Littlehampton brig *Alfred* which was surrounded by broken water on the Lynch. Lifeboatmen were put aboard to assist the crew, and the vessel was taken in to Burry Port.

On Wednesday 22 November 1872 Capt John Jeffreys, master of the brig *Chebucto,* appeared before a Board of Trade inquiry into the loss of his vessel. The inquiry was held at the Guildhall, Swansea before J.T. Jenkin and S.S.H. Horman-Fisher, magistrates, and Capt Harris of London and Lt Elton, chief officer of Mumbles coastguard, nautical assessors. The brig, of 215 tons register and built at Prince Edward Island in 1857, was owned by Chapman Jacobs of Swansea. The vessel left Swansea with 320 tons of patent fuel for Bilbao at noon on 9 November. When it came on to blow the crew complained that the forecastle was leaking and the master put back for Mumbles. The vessel was coming up the coast on the port tack, the wind being west by north. At 6 p.m. Mumbles light was seen ahead and at 6.30 the master asked Thomas Beechy, the mate, whether he had heard the Mixon bell. When told he had not, the master went forward with a glass to look for the buoy. Within a few minutes he could hear the bell and see breakers on the bank. The crew, who were aloft furling the sails. were called to the deck. The vessel struck and seas began to sweep the deck knocking the crew off their feet. They quickly abandoned and called the master and mate to follow or they would leave without them. The two joined the crew and pulled to a schooner which took them to Swansea.

Abraham Ace, keeper of Mumbles lighthouse, had seen the vessel on the shoal and sent James Owen, a gunner at the fort, ashore (it was low water so he walked across the sounds) to inform Coxswain Jenkins. As there was no report of a distress signal, Jenkins went to look for himself and saw the vessel sailing off the land; he correctly decided not to launch. The brig had been abandoned at low water with some of her canvas set and, as the tide made, she came off the bank, sailed herself south and was finally wrecked on the Scarweather. It took the inquiry just half an hour to conclude that the master had been at fault and it suspended his certificate for six months.

Bad storms in years past were often described as being "unequalled within the memory of the oldest inhabitant", but the gale at the end of November 1872 simply exceeded "anything experienced since the *Royal Charter* gale of 1859". On the evening of Saturday the 23rd the Norwegian barque *Pera*, with spruce deals from St Johns, New Brunswick, was driven up channel unmanageable and without a pilot. She went ashore near the wagon works at Port Tennant. The master, his wife and crew of fifteen got ashore but their vessel broke up. Two days later the brig *Paladino*, of Messina, with linseed for Hull, ran up channel seeking shelter but failed to anchor at Mumbles and drove ashore near the infirmary on Swansea foreshore. Coxswain Jenkins found himself short-handed as many of his crew were oyster dredging out of Tenby. When a number of coastguards volunteered, the *Wolverhampton* was launched to the brig's aid. The lifeboat stood by all night and took off the crew of fourteen at dawn. Though she was lying on a sandy bottom, the *Paladino* broke up after a few tides. The same gale drove the Italian barque *Anne* from her anchors but she was taken in tow by the tug *Digby Grand;* and the barque *Antonio Luca*, of Lussin Piccolo, Newcastle to Venice with coal, coke and bricks, was driven up channel and wrecked on Oxwich Point.

Then on Sunday 8 December there was yet another heavy gale. A good deal of damage was caused on shore: in Walter Road, Swansea, the infant child of Rev T.D. Thompson, curate of St Mary's, slept on when the chimneys fell through the roof bringing down the ceilings. The child was found its face blackened by soot, and debris surrounding its cot. The desk at which the curate had sat the evening before to write his sermon was buried by bricks. Mr Rosser, the keeper of the light on Swansea pier, had to crawl along the breakwater to trim the lamps as huge seas swept over it. The barque *Margaret Ann*, of North Shields, Quebec to Swansea with timber, drove ashore just outside the piers. When Mumbles lifeboat arrived, it was blown to leeward, and had to anchor and burn flares to summon further assistance while it rode out the gale. Lt Elton left Mumbles with the rocket apparatus and six coastguards and boarded the tug *Pero Gomez* at the docks. A line was fired from the tug, and after a daring and skilful operation the *Pero Gomez* got alongside the barque and saved all seventeen hands. The vessel was damaged and filled with the tide but she was later refloated and beached off Mumbles to stop her leaks. During the same gale the collier *Hope*, of Maryport, Cork to Swansea in ballast, was driven ashore in Port Eynon Bay. The vessel, which was said to be one hundred years old, quickly broke up but not before her master, Joseph Carmichael, and crew of three had scrambled ashore.

The 320 ton Greek barque *Odysseus*, Salliadis master, ran ashore on Pwll Du Point in thick fog on the evening of 3 March 1873. Her crew got ashore but the vessel, which was on passage from Dublin to Swansea in ballast, became a complete wreck and was sold where she lay.

At 1 a.m. on 23 April the London barque *Nebula*, Fishwick master, ran aground on Port Eynon Point when bound from Antwerp to Cardiff in ballast. The vessel damaged her keel and was holed on the port side under the fore chains, but was quickly repaired and refloated by the tug *Flying Cloud*.

The schooner *Pet*, of Folkestone, was five miles south by east of Worms Head on 12 August when she picked up four men from an open boat. They were Capt Racour and three hands of the *Elizabeth*, of St Malo, bound home with a cargo of coal from Swansea, which had gone down that morning drowning the boy.

The barque *Triton*, with a cargo of salt from Liverpool for her home port of Eckernforde near Kiel, failed to find shelter from a S.W. gale and ran up channel for Mumbles. She struck the Mixon at 4 a.m. on Friday 29 August 1873. The mate and cook took one of the boats but were drowned when it capsized. The tug *Digby Grand*, Capt Daniel Griffiths, saved six men from the rigging of the sunken vessel and the lifeboat *Wolverhampton* went in to coax the last man down from the foretop. The Kaiser awarded an inscribed telescope to Capt Griffiths and a binocular glass to Coxswain Jenkins and these were presented to the men by the German consul at Swansea in October 1874.

COLLISION

Collisions in the crowded anchorage at Mumbles were a common occurrence, but it was rare for vessels to be so badly damaged that they sank, but this is what happened to the Brixham schooner *Dextrous*. She had sailed from Neath on 3 December 1874 and was riding at anchor when the brig *Alfred*, of St Brieuc entered the roads and collided with her. The brig was damaged and towed to Swansea but the schooner quickly began to settle. Her crew boarded the *Aneroid*, which lay near, before landing at Mumbles. The *Dextrous* was soon on the bottom and, as she was a serious hazard to shipping, a lighted buoy marked the wreck until it was cleared.

On the morning of Saturday 2 January 1875 the Swedish schooner *Britannia* ran ashore at Port Eynon in poor visibility. The coastguard were quickly on the scene and persuaded the crew to remain aboard until low water enabled them to walk ashore. Also aboard were William Stevens and William Ley, assistants on the Cardiff pilot cutter *Surprize*, which had foundered off Ilfracombe the evening before. The *Britannia*, which began to break up soon after she ran aground, was bound from le Havre to Cardiff in ballast, and had lost her course in picking the men up.

The Rhosili burial register contains the following entry for the date 27 January 1875: "unknown washed ashore Rhosili Bay". The body was that of a member of the crew of the schooner *Gleaning*, of Bideford, regularly engaged in the limestone trade between Gower and Devon, which had been wrecked with the loss of all hands on Burry Holms three days before.

The Mixon sandbank was the villain once again on 24 June 1875 when the Padstow schooner *Caroline Phillips* was lost with her crew of four.

The Russian barque *Jenny*, Capt Kasteline, Pensacola (Mexico) to Bristol with timber, went ashore below Pilton cliffs during a terrific gale three days before Christmas 1875. It was three in the morning and near high water so the vessel drove well-in allowing the crew to drop onto the rocks from the bowsprit. The *Jenny* was smashed to boards and her cargo and wreckage strewn for miles along the coast from Rhosili to Overton.

WRECK SALE.

PAVILAND, GOWER.

Messrs. **EDWARD ROBEETS & SON**
Have been instructed on behalf of the Underwriters,
TO SELL BY PUBLIC AUCTION,
On the Beach under Paviland and along the Coast,
On MONDAY, JANUARY 3, 1876,
THE whole of the Cargo saved from the wreck of the barque Jenny, from Pensacola, consisting of about 500 LOGS OF SAWN PITCH PINE TIMBER, in lengths from 20 feet to 45 feet by about 1 foot square.
For further particulars apply to Mr. George Gibbs, Lloyd's Agent, Port Eynon; or to the Auctioneers, 6, Picton-place, Swansea.
Sale to commence at Twelve o'clock.—Terms cash.

The Russian barque *Jenny* was smashed to boards when a gale drove her ashore near Paviland in December 1875. (*'The Cambrian'*, Swansea Museum)

George Gibbs arranged the sale of her cargo which was held on 3 January 1876 with auctioneer and purchasers scrambling along the shore where it lay.

A wreck was found bottom-up on the Lynch sand off Whitford on the morning of 28 February 1876. It was identifiied as the Guernsey smack *Reverie*, bound from Cardiff to a French port with coal. Capt Renouf and his crew were drowned.

The barque *France* and the Whitstable brig *Eliza B* had sailed from Swansea on the morning of 13 March 1876. At ten o'clock that evening they collided south of Oxwich during a strong gale which coincided with a spring tide. The barque was badly damaged and her crew, except for the master and one man who was injured and trapped in the wreckage, got aboard the brig. Capt Cotton of the *Eliza B* stood by all night but at dawn the barque had sunk taking the trapped man to his death. The master had been unable to save him and, at the last minute, had abandoned in the boat which was blown up to Mumbles where he was picked up by another vessel.

The 79 ton paddle-tug *Haswell*, owned by Nicholson Bros. of Sunderland, had just left Swansea for home when she ran into a westerly gale and foundered off Oxwich on 8 November 1877. Her crew of eight were picked up by the pilot boat *Benson*. The *Haswell*, built in 1844, had worked as a tug at Swansea since 1849 and during the summer months had doubled as an excursion steamer taking day passengers to Ilfracombe.

The Falmouth barque *Tocapilla*, Bolivia to Swansea with copper ore and regulus, arrived in the channel on 1 January 1878. The weather was foggy but her master, Capt G.W. Wolley, took few soundings and placed too much reliance on his dead reckoning. As a result the vessel ran ashore at

Rhosili on 3 January. The 495 ton vessel remained largely undamaged and was refloated two weeks later. The master's certificate was suspended for three months by the Board of Trade.

On the morning of 10 May 1878 the *Foyle*, of Dublin, was steaming up channel just south of the Helwick when she struck and sank the Swansea pilot boat *Alarm*. Capt Jones and his crew were picked up by the *Foyle* and then transferred to the pilot boat *Benson* which landed them at Swansea.

The steamer *Sully*, of le Havre, stranded at Port Eynon during thick fog on 4 September 1878. As the weather was still summery she became the centre of attraction and the paddle steamer *Velindra* ran excursion trips to see her. The Liverpool Salvage Association was called in, labourers discharged her cargo of minerals, and she was refloated by the steamer *Knight Templar* and docked at Swansea on the evening of the 12th.

The 380 ton barque *Mercur*, of Arendal (Norway), drove ashore at Slade, Port Eynon Bay, before dawn on 21 January 1879. She was bound from Boston, U.S.A., to Penarth for orders with a cargo of maize. The crew got ashore but the vessel became a total loss. A little over a week later the 148 ton brigantine *Sofia*, of and from Naples for Swansea in ballast, was driven ashore in a south-east gale at Longhole Gut between Paviland and Overton. Capt Celendo, his crew of nine and the pilot had a very lucky escape having lost all except the clothes they stood in. Rosser of Wind Street Livery Stables, Swansea, sent down a horse bus to take them to the Sailors' Home.

The ship *Mary Stenhouse*, of Liverpool, 1,246 tons register, ballasted with 350 tons of pig iron, was in tow of the tug *Resolute* from Barrow for Newport. She was manned by a crew of twenty about half of whom were Liverpool runners. The master and mate also had their wives aboard. On the evening of Tuesday 11 February 1879, the tow parted and the vessel ran aground at Rhosili. At 9 p.m. the ship's boat was launched with nine runners and Mrs Hedgcock, the master's wife, aboard. As it made its way to the beach, a heavy ground swell capsized the boat and all ten were drowned. The remaining members of the crew were brought off by the Rhosili L.S.A. under the command of coastguard officer Betts. This was the first service of the rocket company which had been formed in 1877. George Gibbs, Lloyd's agent, was informed of the stranding and rode through the night the twenty five miles to Pembrey. There he arranged for Capt Charles of the tug *Hero* to put to sea and they reached the vessel at 8 a.m. on Wednesday. At high water, shortly before 10 a.m., they got a line secured and the *Mary Stenhouse* was refloated and

---

UNRESERVED WRECK SALE.

Porteynon Bay, near Green Farm, Gower.

Mr. E. HOWARD
WILL SELL BY PUBLIC AUCTION,
On MONDAY, the 10th FEBRUARY, 1879,
At the hour of 12 at noon, at the above place,
THE HULL and MATERIALS of the Norwegian copper fastened barque "MERCUR," as the same may lie at the time of Sale, which will be sold in lots to suit the convenience of purchasers.

The materials consist of anchors, cables, sails, warps, boats, cabin and other stores too numerous to mention.

For further particulars apply to Captain Frivold, Cambrian Hotel, Swansea, or to the Auctioneer, No. 1, Nelson Terrace, Swansea.

Bound from Boston U.S.A. to Penarth with a cargo of maize, the barque *Mercur* was wrecked at Slade on 21 January 1879. (*'The Cambrian'*, Swansea Museum)

towed to Swansea. The Admiralty Court awarded the salvors £400.

The 40 ton sloop *Happy Return*, of Bideford, carrying a cargo of superphosphate from Swansea to Carmarthen, ran onto Port Eynon Point in fog on 19 March 1879 and became a total loss.

On 7 August 1880 a heavy S.W. gale veered to N.W. and blew at force nine. The 105 ton brigantine *Tidy*, of Great Yarmouth, Portland to Llanelli in ballast, was driven ashore in Broughton Bay where she became a wreck after her crew escaped. The veering of the wind caught the Glasgow steamer *Loch Etive* on a lee shore at Rhosili and, to escape, her master slipped the cables at high water and drove his ship over the causeway between the mainland and the Worm.

The barque *Cresswell*, of Newcastle, New South Wales, stranded at Paviland at about 9 a.m. on 27 January 1881. The weather was very thick at the time and the shore breakers had been seen only moments before she struck. The 464 ton vessel was bound in ballast from Liverpool to Cardiff under the command of Capt William Cruse. The master, his wife and three seamen landed but their boat was holed. The remaining crew members waited aboard until taken off by a boat from Port Eynon and the Rhosili L.S.A. The barque became a complete wreck within five hours. At the Board of Trade inquiry, held at the Guildhall, Swansea, it was found that the vessel had been kept on an easterly course after a depth of seventeen fathoms had been found. The master had made no allowance for the effect of the south-east wind on the starboard bow of his light ship (she carried 190 tons of ballast), nor for the effect of the ebb tide, both of which set the vessel towards the shore. Insufficient use had been made of the lead, and a proper lookout had not been kept.

The vessel struck during the mate's watch, but he was having to do the work of a seaman as a number of hands were unfit. The stipendiary magistrate and nautical assessors suspended the master's certificate for three months and the mate's for six.

The 96 ton Weymouth schooner *Geraldine*, bound from Plymouth to Port Eynon with fertiliser, sank in Port Eynon Bay on Wednesday 29 March 1881. Her crew got ashore in the boat, and the wreck was sold by auction on 7 April.

At eight o'clock on the evening of 19 November 1882 the coastguard at Oxwich saw a vessel crossing the bay on a course that would take her dangerously close to Pwll Du Head. Warning signals were fired and the coastguard set off for High Pennard. When they arrived they found the ship *Lammershagen*, of Hamburg, ashore under the Becken at Pwll Du. The 870 ton vessel, Wilhelm Seeth master, was bound to Swansea with a cargo of pitch to load coal for Valparaiso. The master, his crew of nineteen and the "pilot" came ashore in the boats and were put up at the Beaufort Inn in Pwll Du Bay. The pilot, picked up off Ilfracombe, was said to have been the cause of the stranding as he was simply a hobbler. On the ebb tide the master put four hands aboard to protect the property, but the next evening a gale blew up and the vessel began working on the rocks and broke in two. There was a full moon, and during cloud breaks the four men could be seen coming hand over hand along the cable attached to the shore. As the ship worked they were one moment in the water and the next high in the air. Coastguards dashed in to drag the men ashore. A week later fine weather drew crowds to the scene as the wreck and her materials were sold for a total of £500.

LOST WITH ALL HANDS

The events of January 1883 are still talked of by the descendants of those involved at Port Eynon and Mumbles. The first incidents were just the prelude: the Portmadoc schooner *Robert Williams*, Swansea to Abersoch with coal, ran ashore at Slade in dense fog on 6 January. Her crew abandoned and were picked up by another vessel which landed them at Milford. Three days later the 88 ton schooner *Parry's Lodge*, of Beaumaris, Amlwch to Swansea with zinc ore, was wrecked on Pwll Du Point in calm but foggy conditions drowning the master.

The wind had been at near gale force for two days when, at about 4.30 a.m. on Saturday 27 January, it began to blow with tremendous squalls accompanied by rain and hail. The 737 ton Liverpool steamer *Agnes Jack*, John Jones master, had sailed from Mumbles roads at about 3 a.m. She was bound from Cagliari, Sardinia, to Llanelli with silver-bearing lead ore and had sheltered at Mumbles to await the tide. When farm workers left their homes at about 5 a.m. they heard shouts and saw a vessel lying sunk off Port Eynon Point. First light showed about eight men clinging to the vessel's mast. Messengers were sent to Rhosili and Oxwich for the rocket apparatus. Both companies fired rockets but the range was too great. As the tide began to ebb, they were able to move the apparatus out over the rocks but, before further lines could be fired, the mast came down throwing all into the sea. Conditions were so bad that no one made the shore alive. The vessel was identified by her articles which were washed ashore and found intact.

After the inquest had been held at the Ship Inn, the bodies of some of the victims, including that of Philip Beynon the pilot, a native of Llanmadoc but living at Llanelli, were returned to their homes but others were laid to rest in the lower corner of Port Eynon churchyard. A stone still marks their grave bearing the verse

> "Oh had there been a lifeboat there
> To breast the stormy main
> These souls would not have perished thus
> Imploring help in vain."

This wreck prompted an immediate call for a lifeboat to be stationed at Port Eynon. The R.N.L.I. looked favourably on the request and a new station was formed in 1884 with Sam Gibbs as coxswain and Charles Bevan, author of the verse quoted and Lloyd's agent, as resident secretary.

As one tragedy was ending at Port Eynon, another was developing at Mumbles. The barque *Admiral Prinz Adalbert*, of Danzig, Ludwig Leibauer master, was bound from Rochefort to Swansea with 900 tons of pit props. During the squalls she had lost canvas and yards and was becoming unmanageable. The tug *Flying Cloud* failed to tow the vessel into Swansea Bay and she ran onto the rocks of Mumbles Head right below the lighthouse. Mumbles lifeboat *Wolverhampton* was launched, rowed through the sound, and anchored in Bracelet

Bay. John Williams, the bowman, veered the boat towards the wreck and the rescue began. Two German seamen were taken off by breeches buoy, but when the ship's carpenter was being hauled out, a huge sea struck, parted the anchor cable and repeatedly capsized the lifeboat, throwing all but the two Germans into the sea. Two lifeboatmen were saved, as they were driven through the outer sound, by the combined efforts of the lighthouse keeper's daughters, Jessie Ace and Margaret Wright, and an artilleryman from the fort. Coxswain Jenkins and some of his crew struggled onto the rocks but the German carpenter and four lifeboatmen were drowned. The next few tides broke up the vessel and her cargo was washed up for miles around. Later that day the steamship *James Grey* was lost with all hands on the other side of Swansea Bay when it was driven onto the Tusker off Porthcawl.

Just eleven days later on the morning of Wednesday 7 February a bedraggled black labrador was found wandering through Overton. It was the sole survivor of the schooner *Surprise*, of Paimpol, Capt le Tacon, bound to Swansea with 97 tons of pitwood, wrecked below the cliffs to the west of the mere. The wreck was trailing its cables and it was supposed that the vessel had struck the Helwick before losing its anchors. The next day the bodies of four of the crew were found on the beach by William Gibbs, the Port Eynon shoemaker, who was to be appointed bowman of the new lifeboat. The Ship Inn once again witnessed an inquest but on this occasion the bodies were taken up to Swansea for burial in the Catholic section at Danygraig. Concluding its report of this wreck "The Cambrian" commented:

"The number of lives lost on the Glamorgan coast during the last fortnight has now reached the appalling total of fifty three. This is a tale of death and disaster such as has never before been approached, much less equalled, in this district. Living memory holds nothing to compare with it, and local history offers no parallel."

The brigantine *Reine des Fleurs*, of Cannes, homeward bound with coal from Swansea, stranded at West Cross during another heavy gale on 12 February 1883. She broke up and, after the coal had been salvaged, her hull and stores were sold by auction on the spot.

It was not unusual for ship masters to experience trouble with seamen in the few hours after leaving port, for some would have jumped aboard at the last minute and were the worse for drink. Capt Evans, master of the Swansea built and owned barque *Lord Marmion*, put back for Mumbles soon after sailing for Valparaiso when he found able seaman William Price causing trouble in the forecastle. Price was discharged and Capt Evans sent the mate, James McLean, ashore for a replacement. He signed John Strond, a Scandinavian, at the Sailors Home and they travelled to Mumbles by train. The barque left the roads again on the evening of Thursday 29 November 1883 and made her way down channel. When the watches changed at midnight, the vessel was some five miles south of Oxwich Point on the starboard tack, and on a course of south by east under full sail in good clear weather. On being relieved, second mate Elias John drew the first mate's attention to the masthead light of a steamer. The other ship was two miles off and making down channel. Before going below, John checked the barque's lights and found them burning brightly. The second mate's watch had been below a short time when the barque was struck between the fore and main masts by the steamship, the *Jane Bacon*, of Liverpool, which was bound from Bristol to Milford. The steamer's bow cut ten feet or more into the barque which sank within three minutes drowning Capt Evans, an apprentice and three hands. The nine survivors, including both mates and John Strond, were picked up by the steamer's boats. The *Jane Bacon* then made her way slowly to Mumbles towing her boats alongside as her master, Thomas Rowles, feared that she too would go down since she had a large hole in her bows and the fore compartment was flooded. At the Board of Trade inquiry the steamer's lookout admitted that he had neglected his duty by assisting a deckhand with a staysail at the time of the collision. The inquiry found that the lookout and the second mate of the *Jane Bacon*, who was on the bridge, were responsible for the collision but as the latter was uncertificated they could not deal with him.

The 114 ton schooner *Vauban*, of St Malo, was bound from Bordeaux to Cardiff with pitprops. Coming up channel in thick weather, insufficient allowance was made for the south easterly breeze and she ran ashore on 26 December 1883 and was wrecked at the foot of Pennard cliffs.

At 7 p.m. on Tuesday 12 February 1884 the coastguard at Rhosili saw the lights of a vessel close inshore a little to the east of the Worm. Coastguard Darch called out the L.S.A. and made for the cliffs. He found the Norwegian barque *Samuel*, Cardiff to Santos with coal, hard aground and already badly damaged with some of her yards down. Darch fired two rockets but both missed. John Rogers, a young farmer, fired the third and put the line across the vessel. All eleven crew members were soon ashore. A rough road was cut across the cliff to the wreck allowing her cargo to be brought ashore and sold locally.

The pilot boat *J.W.J.*, of Swansea, was run down near the Greengrounds by the steamer *Sea Fisher*, Barrow to Swansea with steel plates, on Thursday 21 May 1885. Pilots David Tamlyn and John Bevan and the two hobblers got aboard the ship; the pilot boat was taken in tow but sank before getting into shallow water.

Five men struggled ashore from the barque *René*, of Nantes, wrecked at Overton on the morning of 8 January 1886. The vessel had left Cardiff with 450 tons of coal for Arcachon on the 7th and anchored off Nash Point that evening. Resuming her passage on the ebb tide, the weather became thick and stormy and the vessel struck heavily on the Helwick. The barque was driven ashore at about 2 a.m. and quickly broke up. The crew either jumped or were washed overboard but the master, two seamen and the fifteen year old boy were drowned. The survivors were taken in by farmer John Bevan, and when the bodies of their shipmates were recovered the inquest was held at his house. Once again the victims were buried at Danygraig, Swansea.

A month later the Port Eynon lifeboat crew assembled when a schooner was seen aground inside Port Eynon Point. The vessel's crew got ashore in their boat so that the lifeboat was not required. She was the *Hope*, of Newport, bound to New Ross, Co. Wexford, with coal. Though badly damaged she was eventually refloated and repaired.

The Aberystwyth brig *Xanthippe*, Jamaica to Port Talbot with phosphate rock, ran aground on the west side of Oxwich Point in thick fog at about 4 a.m. on 20 March 1886. The crew abandoned and got ashore in their boats. As the tide fell, the vessel

The *Agnes*, of West Hartlepool, went ashore at Whiteshell Point, Caswell, on 8 October 1886, and broke up in a severe gale a week later. *(A James Andrews photo, Gareth Mills collection)*

heeled over, her yards struck the rocks and she became a total loss.

The steamship *Agnes*, of West Hartlepool, Rouen to Swansea, went ashore at Whiteshell Point (east of Caswell) at 3 a.m. on Friday 8 October 1886. It was foggy but calm and the crew got ashore safely. The ship was made watertight and pumped out, but when she refloated there were no tugs in attendance so that she again went ashore and was badly damaged. A week later she was pounded to pieces by the south-west storm which wrecked a number of vessels in other parts of the channel. Her hull and machinery were sold to John Hurley, the Bristol shipbreaker for £272, and her compasses and boat raised £33. The storm of Friday 15 October caused a fatality at Mumbles: William Walkey the signalman at Lloyd's signal station at the lighthouse, was crossing the outer sound with a parcel of groceries. The tide was up to his knees when the wind whipped the parcel from his grasp and he fell in trying to recover it. A sea swept him away and when the two keepers launched a boat to go to his aid it was smashed to pieces.

The schooner *Thames*, of London, sailed from Port Talbot with a general cargo for Bilbao. She struck the Scarweather in fog, drifted north, and foundered off Mumbles Head on the evening of 20 November 1886. Her crew got ashore in safety. As the wreck constituted a hazard to navigation, it was marked by a lighted wreck buoy. Trinity House had the wreck and its cargo raised the following year and they were disposed of by a series of auctions held in Swansea.

A southerly gale on the night of 18 January 1887 drove the 52 ton sloop *Argus*, Lannion to Cardiff with potatoes, ashore at Llangennith. The crew got ashore though the master was badly injured and the vessel became a total loss.

The Port Eynon lifeboatmen made their first service launch on 22 March 1887 when a brig was seen stranded on Oxwich Point. When Sam Gibbs and his crew arrived in the lifeboat, *A Daughter's Offering*, they found that the crew of the *Prophete Elie*, of Nantes, had got safely ashore and their services were not required. The brig became a total loss.

The steamship *Ashdale*, of Glasgow, Capt Hamilton, France to Mumbles for orders, ran ashore on Port Eynon Point in thick fog on the morning of Saturday 7 May 1887. At day break, it was found that she had lost her rudder and stern-post but was otherwise sound. Charles Bevan, lifeboat secretary and Lloyd's agent, went up to Swansea to arrange for the tug *Challenger* to tow her off and she was taken to Mumbles on Sunday evening.

Local people and holidaymakers are familiar with the wooden wreck on the beach at Rhosili. This is all that remains of the barque *Helvetia*, of Horten (Norway), bound from Campbelton (New Brunswick) to Swansea with deals. The vessel arrived off Mumbles on the night of Monday 31 October 1887 and Capt Stevensen ordered signals to be burnt for a pilot. A fresh breeze sprang up from south-east and he was obliged to stand down channel. At 8 a.m. on Tuesday the vessel was abreast the Helwick when the wind freshened to a gale and veered to south-west. The barque was labouring heavily and drifting shorewards. She drifted over the bank losing part of her deck load and ran around the Worm to anchor in Rhosili Bay. At low water she struck heavily and the coastguard called out the L.S.A. One man was brought ashore by the breeches buoy, but the rest came ashore in

Gower's best known wreck lies on Rhosili beach. She was the Norwegian barque *Helvetia*, with a cargo of timber for Swansea, driven from her anchors on 1 November 1887. *(Author's photo)*

their boats when the tide made. The vessel seemed to be riding comfortably to her cables but the wind went round to the west and at 5.30 p.m. she parted and drove onto the beach where her remains still lie. About 500 tons of cargo were salvaged and the wreck was stripped of everything saleable.

The small Llanelli steamer *Cambria* was involved in salvaging materials from the *Helvetia*, and on Saturday 21 January 1888 she was beached alongside the wreck. On the flood the wind rose to a gale driving the steamer broadside onto the beach. The L.S.A. put a line over her and one member of the crew came ashore. The vessel was later refloated by running a cable out to an anchor dropped off shore and kedging herself off. Unfortunately she managed to lose the anchor in the process. Two months later on Sunday 18 March the *Cambria's* master, John Hopkins, decided to recover the anchor. At low water it was lashed below their boat and the chain cable placed in the boat. Naturally with six men aboard, the boat was low in the water and as they rowed out it was obvious that she would sink. Letting the anchor go, the boat capsized throwing all into the sea. Farmer George Thomas was tending his sheep when he heard their shouts. Looking up he saw one man swimming ashore and the boat drifting out with two clinging to its bottom. Thomas was joined by coastguard Finlay and William Richards. They found that William Thomas had now reached the beach and lay exhausted in the shallows. Having assisted

him, they made their way out over the causeway which was being covered by the tide. They recovered the upturned boat but there was no sign of other survivors: Capt Hopkins and four had drowned.

In the meantime there had been another stranding near Port Eynon. At 6 p.m. on 13 January 1888 a ship's siren was heard through dense fog. Shortly afterwards a report was received that a steamer was ashore at Slade's Foot, Overton. The maroons were fired and Coxswain Sam Gibbs led the lifeboat crew in rescuing eleven men from the 1,400 ton *Milan,* of Hull, carrying a cargo of cotton seed from

This sketch, by Tottenham Lucas son of the rector of Rhosili, shows the Llanelli steamer *Cambria* salvaging the cargo of the wrecked *Helvetia. (Robert Lucas collection)*

Alexandria to Bristol. The Rhosili L.S.A. was also called out and put a line across the ship to bring the remaining ten crew ashore by breeches buoy.

Next day it was found that the ship was badly damaged and had nine feet of water in her holds. Charles Bevan informed Lloyd's and Capt Toyer a salvage expert was sent down. After ten days work 500 tons of cargo had been discharged. The Dundee Salvage Association then employed the Swansea Drydock and Engineering Co. to repair the hull and to blast away the rocks surrounding the ship. The *Milan* was refloated on Monday 30 January by the tugs *Privateer* and *Flying Cloud* and, after being beached at Port Eynon and later at Mumbles, the tow to Bristol for further repairs began on 3

The remains of the iron-hulled barque *Vennerne*, of Sonderho (Denmark), below the cliffs at Rhosili. *(Author's photo)*

February. Milan Cottage at Overton, for many years the home of Charles Bevan, was named after this ship.

A Board of Trade inquiry into the stranding was held at the Townhall, Hull, on 18 February. The *Milan's* master, Capt Lowery, and chief mate Hanson (son-in-law of the proprietors of the Caswell Bay Hotel) gave evidence: At 2.30 a.m. on 13 January they had been abreast of the Longships (off Lands End) in clear weather. Thereafter there was thick fog. At 1.50 p.m. land was seen one mile off the starboard bow and a lighthouse could be seen on a headland. They agreed that it was Hartland Point. At 4.15 they hove to and found bottom in a little over twenty fathoms. Believing that they were in mid-channel, they proceeded cautiously through the fog and the master went to tea leaving the mate on the bridge. At 5.35 the mate saw land ahead and called for full speed astern but the ship ran onto the rocks west of Overton. The nautical assessors found that the stranding was attributable to the master having mistaken the north end of Lundy for Hartland Point. He was to blame in not having taken further measures to make a positive identification of the headland but, as his conduct fell short of a default, he was allowed to keep his certificate.

The steam trawler *Jane*, of Falmouth, parted her cables off Port Eynon and was driven onto the sandy beach on 2 May 1888. Her crew of two got ashore with just a soaking and were taken in by Coxswain Gibbs. Two weeks later the trawler was refloated by the tug *Cambrian*. Meanwhile the Padstow brigantine *Henry Edmunds* was wrecked at the foot of Overton cliffs on the morning of 8 May while bound to Swansea in ballast. Her crew also survived.

FOG

Though "rock, tempest, fire and foe" may have been regarded as the greatest dangers to be faced by shipping, fog too was a formidable hazard as the number of casualties caused by it has already demonstrated. Fog signals were used at Mumbles lighthouse and on the Helwick lightship, but the rest of the peninsula was unprotected in this way and numerous strandings resulted. It is perhaps surprising that Port Eynon and Oxwich Points were not provided with fog signals.

The steamship *Benamain*, of London, left Swansea on 28 March 1890 with a general cargo of about 400 tons including 50 tons of copper ingots for le Tréport. At 4.10 p.m. she was steaming at 6 knots when she stranded in fog on the east side of Lundy. She refloated at 9 a.m. next day but foundered about seven miles off Mumbles that evening while returning to Swansea. Her crew of twelve were picked up by the pilot boat *Rival* and landed at Swansea. The Board of Trade inquiry found that she was insufficiently manned, and that the master had not made allowance for the ebb tide setting the vessel towards the island. His certificate was suspended for six months. Though a salvage operation was reported to have begun two years later, divers who have recently discovered the wreck a few miles off Pwll Du believe that her cargo is intact.

The Cork brigantine *Sarsfield* was bound in ballast for Newport when it entered thick banks of fog in the early hours of Sunday 11 January 1891. None of the channel lights were seen, and when the mist lifted the headland they saw was thought to be Hartland Point. Unfortunately they had seen the Worm and were soon ashore a little north of Diles Lake on Rhosili Beach. Capt Macdonell, his wife and crew of five got ashore. The crew were put up at the King's Head, Llangennith, while Captain and Mrs Macdonell lodged with the Helme family at Hillend. They were able to save their belongings and some of the vessel's materials, but the *Sarsfield* became a wreck.

On the evening of Sunday 1 March 1891, the 120 ton brigantine *H.L.C.*, of le Havre, Port Talbot to Pornic with coal, grounded on the Mixon in fog. Her crew got ashore but the vessel broke up on the next tide.

The Port Eynon lifeboat was launched on 23 December 1891 when a brig was seen aground on Oxwich Point. When Sam Gibbs and his crew arrived they found that their services were not required as the vessel's men had got ashore. The brig, the 220 ton *Felicité*, of Vannes, Nantes to Swansea with pit props, became a total loss.

The Milford ketch *Favourite* was disabled by a heavy gale on 16 November 1893. By the next day she had drifted to a point three miles off Worms Head where the mate left in the boat and rowed up the coast. The Port Eynon lifeboat was launched and brought him ashore. The master and a seaman were taken off the ketch shortly before it foundered and landed at Swansea by the schooner *Jeune Charles*.

The barque *Althea*, of Grimstad (Norway),

The barque *Duisberg*, with a cargo of timber from Nova Scotia, became a complete wreck after stranding on Oxwich Point on 11 November 1899. The vessel's windmill pump is seen on the deck. *(Gareth Mills collection)*

Swansea to Christiania with coal, had been weather bound at Mumbles for two weeks. When her master was ashore on 13 December 1893, a gale blew up, and the vessel dragged her anchors out into the channel and became unmanageable. She drifted down channel and drove ashore at Nicholaston Pill, Oxwich. The Port Eynon lifeboat crew were alerted and they launched with great difficulty due to the huge seas breaking on the shore. After a hard struggle at the oars they were able to make sail and arrived to find the 492 ton vessel a wreck. The crew of eleven had abandoned and were in the boat which pitched and rolled alongside. All were taken aboard the lifeboat and landed at Port Eynon.

On the morning of 22 March 1894 a schooner was seen to miss stays and go ashore at Longhole Gut to the west of Overton. Her crew were seen trying to launch the boat from the wildly pitching deck, and a message was sent to Port Eynon for the lifeboat to make a quick launch. As Sam Gibbs and his crew approached the wreck they were hailed by the crew of another schooner, the *Jane Shearer*, of Greenock, which had picked up the crew of three after they had pulled out to sea away from the heavy seas at the cliff face. The stranded vessel was the *Glenravil Miner*, of Barrow, with a cargo of pitch which was scattered over the rocks when she broke up.

The 375 ton barque *Vennerne*, of Sonderho (Denmark), was in ballast from Aberdovey for Swansea when she sought shelter inside the Worm at Rhosili on 24 October 1894. After straining at her cables for some hours, they parted and she drove onto the beach close under the cliffs. The Rhosili rocket company were quickly on the scene and fired four lines but Capt Aare, his wife, child, and crew of seven abandoned in the boat. As there was every chance of capsizing in the surf, the master made a line fast to the vessel and veered his boat onto the beach where members of the rocket company led by coastguards Finlay, Grove and Taylor helped them ashore. The next day the tug *Privateer* failed in an attempt to refloat the vessel and it became a wreck. The remains were sold by auction conducted by R.O. Jones of the firm of Beynon and Meager on 2 November; the iron hull went to Barlow of Swansea for £54. Parts of the wreck, known locally as the *Vernani*, may still be seen on the beach at Old Castle corner.

There were a number of incidents in 1895, two being very serious. The first was on Saturday 20 April. At about 3.15 a.m., as the pilot boat *Mary* was putting Capt Tamlin aboard a vessel in Mumbles roads, a loud crash was heard to the west. The *Mary* went directly to the scene and found the 400 ton Glasgow steamer *Severn* cruis-

ing around. When hailed they were told that there had been a collision with a tug which had sunk rapidly without survivors. The steamer made her way to the roads and the master, Capt McDougall, went to Swansea to report to the authorities. As a number of tugs were out "seeking" it was some time before it was realised that it was the locally-owned

The steamer *Lillian*, Tunis to Swansea with calamine, silver and lead ores, stranded on Mumbles Head on 6 July 1906. She was refloated three days later. *(Gareth Mills collection)*

Wasp which was missing with her crew of Henry Beynon mate, James Jones engineer, and David Morgan fireman. It was also believed that George Tosh, a friend of the crew, was aboard. The tug's master, Robert Jones, was on leave. The tugs *Cambria* and *Fawn* swept the area a few days later, and discovered an obstruction less than a mile west of the Mixon buoy in about twelve fathoms. Ned Stroud, the Harbour Trust diver, went down during the middle of May and reported that the *Wasp* was on her keel with a slight list to port. She was lying roughly east-west with her bows towards Mumbles. The Board of Trade inquiry into the loss heard that the tug had left port at about 11 p.m. on 19 April and the *Severn* at 2.45 the next morning. As the tug was crossing the steamer's course she should have kept out of her way. The steamer's side lights, though lit, were found to be in "a somewhat defective condition". Though Capt McDougall was in default his certificate was

The *Janet*, Port Eynon's second lifeboat, was at the station for ten years. She performed three rescues but capsized on service in January 1916 with the loss of her coxswain and two lifeboatmen. *(Michael Gibbs collection)*

returned to him. The wreck was raised and beached on the mud flats in front of the George Hotel, Mumbles, on the evening of 23 June. Huge crowds were drawn to the scene, some waded out to get a closer look, and local boatmen did a roaring trade at sixpence a trip. By dark the bodies of James Jones and David Morgan had been recovered, and taken to the stable of the George to await an inquest.

The Llanelli and Burry Port pilot cutters *Smiling Morn* and *Maria* were anchored inside Worms Head on the morning of Tuesday 1 October 1895 when a westerly gale blew up. The vessels dragged their anchors and the *Smiling Morn* drove across the *Maria's* bows. The vessels collided, were both holed and sank. Both crews abandoned and got ashore safely.

At a few minutes past midnight on the morning of Friday 4 October the maroons were fired at Mumbles to summon the lifeboat crew. The alarm had been raised by Ann Ace, wife of the lighthouse keeper, and Mrs Williams, wife of the assistant keeper, who had seen a vessel on the Mixon. There was some delay in forming a crew, but when the lifeboat got afloat it was towed to the scene by the tug *Privateer*. The vessel had struck the western end of the bank and as the lifeboat approached, Coxswain John Williams saw the fore and main masts go overboard. The wreck was engulfed by huge seas, there was wreckage everywhere, but no sign of survivors. The tug and lifeboat made as thorough a search as conditions would allow but no one was found. A few days later William Jenkins of Clifton Terrace, Mumbles, found a body floating through the moorings off the village. The inquest held at the Pilot Inn heard that it had been identified as that of Patrick Colford, master of the 158 ton Waterford brigantine *Zoe* which had been bound from Liverpool to Swansea with pitch.

The 1,272 ton steamship *Imbros*, of Hull, stranded on the Helwick in fog on 2 February 1897. Bound from the Black Sea to Swansea with grain, she was beached at Mumbles where her cargo was discharged into lighters. Lloyd's surveyor declared the vessel a constructive total loss and she was towed to Cardiff for breaking.

The Rev John Ponsonby Lucas, Rector of Rhosili, writing to his son Loftus (a master mariner) from the rectory above Rhosili beach described the excitement of the first Sunday of February 1898: "as I issued from the back gate for Rhosili service, coming down Rolling Tor for a long way on the path I, to my infinite astonishment, saw an immense crowd, a long procession of people coming along. I could not imagine what it meant. However I soon perceived the rocket apparatus on the lower road, so I saw at once the meaning of it. A steamer of 2,000 tons the *Marshal Keith*, from Dieppe to Llanelli, had stuck on a sandbank opposite Broughton Bay. As I met the people I said I might as well go home! It being Sunday and there being no little excitement here, everybody, men, women and all the children were there. I officiated in an almost empty church. Well the said steamship, as the tide rose, got off all right so all the people returned home like, in a manner, bad pennies! It is very odd but that sort of thing so often happens on a Sunday."

The ketch *Three Sisters*, of Cardigan, left Port Talbot on the morning of 5 July 1899 with coal for Llangranog. Her master, John Thomas of Trevor, Aberporth, put in to Mumbles roads to wait for the ebb and left there at 3.30 p.m. As they were beating down channel, the weather became thick and they put about to return to Mumbles. Off the Greengrounds buoy, the fog became very thick and they were in collision with the steamship *Tweed*, which had just left Swansea for the Clyde. As soon as the ketch was seen, Capt White of the *Tweed* ordered the helm hard a'port and the engines reversed, but the ketch seemed to broach-to across the steamer's bows and was cut in two trapping the master between the tiller and gunwhale. Capt Thomas freed himself as the vessel went down and

was picked up by a boat from the steamer. His crew, his son David aged sixteen, and nineteen year old David Mathias of Ty Mawr, Aberporth, were drowned. When their bodies were recovered they were taken to Aberporth and interred there at St Cynwyl's church.

The 969 ton barque *Duisberg*, of Christiania (Norway), was sixty days out of Parrsboro (Nova Scotia) with timber, bound to Mumbles for orders, when she stranded on Oxwich Point on the morning

The Austrian steamship *Epidauro* ashore near Overton in February 1913. *(M. A. Clare, author's collection)*

of Saturday 11 November 1899. The vessel had been leaking badly for weeks and the windmill pump was unable to cope. As a result the crew were exhausted by their exertions at the pumps, and by the dwindling provisions on the prolonged crossing. The vessel began to break up in the heavy seas which ran onto the rock shelf of the point. When Sam Gibbs and the crew of the lifeboat *A Daughter's Offering* arrived from Port Eynon they found the vessel's fore and main masts gone by the board and the crew safely ashore. By four that afternoon the tide had ebbed sufficiently for the crew to return aboard to get their belongings. The timber cargo was salvaged but the barque became a total loss.

Tugs were summoned from Swansea when a large steamship was reported stranded on Oxwich Point on the morning of Saturday 23 February 1900. She was the 1,600 ton *Ethiopia*, of London, in ballast from Hamburg for Port Talbot with a crew of thirty six. The tugs failed to tow her clear and low tide showed the hull badly strained with water pouring from the plates. The following Tuesday the Liverpool salvage vessel *Ranger* arrived and, after a days work, the *Ethiopia* was refloated and dry-docked at Port Talbot.

The steam collier *St Vincent* was able to proceed after refloating herself from the Dangers reef at Rhosili on 17 May 1900. However the following month the tiny *Tivyside* became a total loss when she stranded at Overton. In ballast from Carmarthen to Bristol under the command of Capt Harvey, the 67 ton iron-hulled screw steamer, owned by John Bacon and Co. of Liverpool, ran ashore on the morning of Friday 15 June in thick fog. The Rhosili and Oxwich rocket companies attended but the crew of six and the seven passen-

gers got ashore in the boat. By high water, only her masts and funnel could be seen.

A severe westerly gale struck the peninsula on Thursday 10 September 1903. During the afternoon, the schooner *Glenfeadon* parted her cables at Mumbles and drove ashore near the lifeboat house; she was refloated the next day by the tug *Falcon*. After the storm, Rhosili beach was found to be strewn with wreckage which included the stern of the *J.K. Allport*, of Plymouth. Two weeks later bodies were washed up on Swansea beach, at Port Eynon and Three Cliffs. One was identified by a pawn ticket found in his pocket. In the waistcoat pocket of another was a small box containing a memorial notice for Edward Shannon who had died in the Kingstown (Dun Laoghaire) lifeboat disaster of Christmas Eve 1895. Both were members of the crew of the *S.S. Ierne* which had left Newport on 10 September with coal for Dublin. It was assumed that the vessel had been overwhelmed by the storm and had foundered off Gower. In August 1992 a group of experienced divers located the wreck of the *Ierne* near the Scarweather sandbank and recovered its bell.

The ketch *Bristol Packet* had discharged part of her cargo of fertiliser onto the beach at Port Eynon, and was due to sail around to Oxwich, when a gale came up on Wednesday 12 April 1905 driving her ashore on the evening tide. She became a wreck.

The tug *Indefatigable*, of Swansea, ran aground on the rock shelf below Whiteshell Point in thick fog on the morning of Tuesday 23 January 1906. The crew were in no danger and were able to get ashore at low water. Hopes of refloating the vessel were high, but her port bow was holed two days later and she was abandoned.

The ketch *Tilly*, of Gloucester, was carrying a

The 280 ton *Bluebell* ashore near Culverhole after stranding in fog on 15 February 1913. *(Gareth Mills collection0*

cargo of crushed granite from Falmouth to Sharpness when she sprang a leak on Friday 21 December 1906. Capt Jones, his son and seaman Jacob Tandy worked at the pumps but were forced to abandon when the water gained on them. The ketch foundered a mile and a half off the Helwick and her crew were picked up by the *S.S. Ragusa* and landed at Swansea.

The 180 ton brigantine *Marie Therese*, Arcachon to Swansea with pitwood, struck the western end of the Helwick in fog on the night of Saturday 19 January 1907. She was abandoned in a sinking condition while Capt Antin and his crew of seven rowed to Tenby.

Shortly before five o'clock on the morning of Monday 10 June 1907 a small boat was seen in the entrance channel to Swansea docks making its way laboriously through the wind and rain. Aboard were Capt Duval, his wife, three men and the boy of the 160 ton schooner *Bougainville*, of Lannion. They

Scrapping the *Epidauro*. The hull of the ship can be seen on the right. In the foreground is the railway used to carry the scrap away.
(M. A. Clare, author's collection)

had sailed from Swansea on 7 June with a cargo of patent fuel. Sixty miles south-west of Lundy the vessel sprang a leak and they put back pumping continuously. The crew were forced to abandon four miles off Oxwich Point at 10.45 on Sunday evening and watched her go down in twenty minutes.

On 22 November that year the ketch *Jane*, of Aberystwyth, Aberaeron to Port Talbot in ballast, was driven into Pwll Du Bay by a southerly gale.

Her crew of master and mate got ashore but the vessel broke up.

The ketch *Notre Dame de Lourdes*, with a cargo of pit props for Llanelli, drove ashore on Rhosili beach a little south of Burry Holms on Friday 15 April 1910. Her crew got ashore and were lodged in local farms. Though on a sandy beach, the vessel broke her back after a few tides.

The 136 ton schooner *Wiln*, of Fowey, was bound from Devonport to Llanelli with steel scrap

Recovering the boiler of the *Epidauro. (M. A. Clare, author's collection)*

Scrapping the *Epidauro*. The foreman has been rabbiting and proudly shows off his bag. *(M. A. Clare, author's collection)*

and arrived off the Burry estuary on the afternoon of 28 January 1911 some hours before the flood would allow her to enter. Her master, Thomas Rowe, decided to stand off, but that evening the schooner was in collision with the Liverpool steamship *Irena*, Briton Ferry to Dublin with coal. The steamer launched her boat and saved three from the water but one died of exposure. The master and two others had gone down with the vessel.

During a furious gale on the afternoon of Monday 30 October 1911, signals were sent up by the Helwick lightship. The Tenby and Port Eynon lifeboat stations were informed and both boats launched. The *Janet* had a hard beat to windward under reefed lugsail, but the Tenby boat had an easier passage. They reached the lightship at around 6 p.m. and were told that shortly before three o'clock a schooner had been seen to founder two miles to the south. Both boats searched and found a good deal of floating wreckage but no sign

The ketch *Leonora* beached at Rotherslade on 19 November 1913 after colliding with the tug *Atlas. (M. A. Clare, author's collection)*

of life. Later two bodies and a seaman's chest were recovered and helped to identify the lost vessel as the 100 ton brigantine *Sicie* which had sailed from Swansea with coal for Lorient on the 28th.

The 2,000 ton Cunarder *Veria*, of Liverpool, was coming up channel on the evening of 17 February 1912 bound for Swansea. At 11 p.m. the vessel was off Port Eynon steering east and making eight knots when lights were seen ahead. Twelve minutes later third officer Finlow, who was on the bridge, saw a small vessel crossing their course. He ordered full speed astern and the wheel hard a'port. Hearing the three short blasts on the siren to indicate full speed astern, Capt George Jefferies ran up onto the bridge to catch a glimpse of the vessel being struck and capsizing. The *Veria* stopped engines, threw lifebelts over the side and lowered a boat. They searched for an hour and a half but found nothing and steamed up to Swansea to report the incident. It soon became evident that the vessel sunk was the Swansea tug *Charioteer* and that all hands were lost. They were Fred Evans of Orchard Street, the master; R. Pritchard of Odo Street, Hafod, mate; Tom Gow of Bond Street, the engineer; fireman R. Williams; and W. Griffiths the deckhand of Rodney Street, Swansea.

The trawler *Picton Castle*, skippered by Joseph Rust of Mumbles, was returning from a fishing trip on 5 September 1912. A strong westerly gale was blowing and, as they steamed up channel off Oxwich, they saw a schooner swamped by huge seas and capsize. The trawler launched her boat and rescued Capt Birzonarn, four hands and the dog from the *Espérance* which was bound from Boulogne to Swansea with pitwood. Skipper Rust and his crew were honoured by the French government for their swift action.

The *Leonora* breaking up in a gale the day after she was beached. *(M. A. Clare, author's collection)*

A little after dawn on 13 February 1913 a ship's boat pulled ashore to land four men near the lifeboat house at Port Eynon. They were the mate, engineer and two seamen of the 1,200 ton Austrian steamship *Epidauro,* of Lussin-Piccolo. Their ship, bound from Genoa to Swansea in ballast, had gone ashore in thick fog at Washslade to the west of Overton. The maroons were fired and the lifeboat *Janet* launched with Billy Gibbs at the helm. Lifeboat honorary secretary Charles Bevan, and the bowman, Frank Taylor, arrived after the boat had gone and walked over the cliffs to the scene of the stranding with the four Austrians. There they boarded another of the ship's boats which took them out to the vessel. Three of the men had climbed aboard, when a heavy swell capsized the boat. Bevan clung to the ladder, but Taylor and two seamen were thrown into the sea. The *Janet* arrived just in time to save them. The lifeboat stood by the *Epidauro* until the ebb allowed her crew to walk ashore. The Rhosili L.S.A. company arrived, got a line over the ship, and rigged up the breeches buoy. This was left in place as the ship's master, Capt Bete, remained on board overnight. Within a few days it was realised that the vessel could not be refloated and she was broken up where she lay.

Just two days after this stranding, Charles Bevan, who lived at Overton, was roused from sleep at 4.30 a.m. by a ship's siren and distress rockets. Investigating, he found another ship ashore near Culverhole on the east side of Overton Mere. The *Janet* was launched in thick fog and saved all twelve crew of the *Bluebell,* of Manchester, bound from Partington to Swansea with 600 tons of coal for the Swansea Gas Company. Later that day Bevan, who was also local agent of the Shipwrecked Mariners' Society, sent the twelve men to Swansea by motor bus. The 280 ton *Bluebell* also became a total loss.

On the morning of 19 November 1913 the Cardiff tug *Atlas* collided with the ketch *Leonora,* which was carrying a cargo of coal from Swansea to Barnstaple. The badly damaged ketch was abandoned by her crew who rowed ashore at Mumbles. The *Leonora* drifted ashore at Rotherslade and broke up in heavy weather the next day. Just two days later the steamship *Merthyr* ran ashore on Oxwich beach in fog but refloated on the next tide and was able to proceed.

LIFEBOAT DISASTER

At about 6.40 p.m. on Saturday 17 October 1914 there was a collision near the Helwick lightship between the *S.S. Corundum*, Burry Port to Rouen with 1,600 tons of coal, and the *S.S. Kyleness*, Swansea to Liverpool with 6,000 tons of coal. The former vessel quickly foundered and its crew were picked up by the *Kyleness* which returned to Swansea with its bows stove in.

The Wexford schooner *Elizabeth Jane*, which had been sheltering in Mumbles roads for some days, fired distress signals on the evening of 27 December 1915. A heavy gale was blowing and the pilot cutter *Beaufort*, which was in the bay, signalled for the lifeboat and made for the scene at full speed. When the *Beaufort* and lifeboat arrived, the vessel was sinking in huge seas. Lines were thrown to men in the rigging but they were overwhelmed and there were no survivors. The weather was still bad five days later on 1 January 1916 driving the *S.S. Dunvegan* ashore at Pennard when she suffered engine failure. The alarm was raised soon after 10 a.m. and the Port Eynon lifeboat, *Janet*, was launched in dreadful conditions. She arrived off Pennard and found the ship close-in and surrounded by broken water. Coxswain Billy Gibbs anchored off to await better conditions. When he could see that the breeches buoy had been set up and that the ship's crew were safe, Coxswain Gibbs decided to return to station. After weighing anchor, the lifeboat was caught on the starboard quarter by a big sea and capsized, throwing her crew into the water. The boat righted, and the crew dragged

themselves aboard only to find that the second coxswain, William Eynon, and lifeboatman George Harris were missing. As they searched for them the boat was once again capsized and this time Coxswain Gibbs was swept away. Unable to find their comrades or to get back to Port Eynon, the survivors allowed the boat to drift up towards Mumbles where they landed next morning. The *Dunvegan* was refloated a few days later with little damage and safely docked at Swansea. The R.N.L.I. decided to close the Port Eynon station after this tragedy as the larger Tenby and Mumbles lifeboats would be able to cover the area.

The Swedish ship *Mercia*, Bilbao to Briton Ferry with iron ore, ran aground at Pennard during a blinding snowstorm on the evening of 29 February 1916. The pilot cutter *Beaufort*, and the Swansea tug *Trusty*, failed to refloat her, and she was abandoned to the underwriters when she broke up two days later. Her valuable cargo was salvaged later that year.

A storm of near hurricane force, accompanied by heavy snow, during the early hours of 28 March 1916 parted the 260 ton Russian schooner *Olga* from her anchors and swept her onto Mumbles Head. The crew landed at about 4.30 a.m. assisted by the lighthouse keepers. The *Olga*, Moss Point, Mississippi, for Swansea with pit props, was refloated but declared a constructive total loss and sold for breaking.

The barque *Tridonia*, of London, 1,981 tons, was a former German vessel seized in a British port

The barque *Tridonia*, of London, on the rock ledges west of Oxwich Point. Her master and two men were drowned. *(W. T. Goldsworthy collection)*

The steam-hopper *Franklin* foundered off Mumbles Head on 24 October 1917 drowning four of her crew. She is seen here being raised the following April by three salvage vessels. *(M. A. Clare, author's collection)*

at the outbreak of war. On passage, in ballast, from Dublin to Buenos Aires, she met a severe gale, lost canvas, and was driven unmanageable into the Bristol Channel. She was anchored off Port Eynon on Sunday 29 October 1916 and made signals for a pilot. The steam pilot cutter *Beaufort* put Capt William Davies aboard on the fourth attempt, and offered to tow the vessel up the coast, but this was refused by the master, Capt Stewart. Capt Davies advised that springs should be fitted to the anchor cables and this was done. At midday on Monday the springs parted, quickly followed by the port cable and then the starboard. The signal flags NC were hoisted, to show that the vessel was not under command, and she drove ashore bow first to the west of Oxwich Point at low water, about 2 p.m. Charles Bevan was quickly on the scene and messages were sent for the Oxwich and Rhosili rocket companies. Capt Stewart called all hands, including his wife, to the weather side fearing that the masts would go by the board. The mate, carpenter and two seamen attempted to bring a line ashore, but their boat capsized and they were fortunate to reach the shore alive. On the evening tide the stern and much of the main deck were swept by huge seas and the crew and Mrs Stewart sought refuge on the forecastle and jib boom. The second mate, J. Rock of Chester, panicked and locked himself in a deck house and was drowned along with the master who had gone to assist him. A seaman, Patrick Russell of Dublin, was also lost and lies buried in Oxwich churchyard.

The rocket brigades were eventually successful in getting a line over the vessel and twenty survivors, including the pilot and Mrs Stewart, were brought ashore on Tuesday morning. A group of Swansea pilots went to Oxwich by motor car with spare clothes and took Capt Davies home that evening. The crew and Mrs Stewart lodged at Oxwich overnight and travelled up to Swansea on Wednesday.

A south-east gale struck on the evening of 16 November 1916 and next morning the 200 ton

Pumping out the *Franklin* beached at Mumbles in April 1918. *(M. A. Clare, author's collection)*

schooner *St Christophe*, Blaye (near Bordeaux) for Swansea with pitwood, began dragging her anchors. Shortly before noon, she was on the Cherrystone at Mumbles Head. With the tide on the ebb and a rough sea, she settled and began to break up. Lighthouse keeper John Thomas and his assistant, Charles Cottle, organised the garrison of Mumbles Head fort in the rescue effort. A line was floated in and retrieved by a human chain who then hauled a heavier cable from the wreck. Capt Francis Poquet and his crew of seven came hand over hand along the cable. They had given their dog a piece of wood and he jumped in and swam ashore with it in his mouth.

Two French vessels fell victim to mines off Gower at the end of December 1916. On the 26th the *Saint Louis*, Bordeaux to Swansea, struck a mine off Mumbles Head and sank with the loss of her crew of three. The following day the *Paul Paix* arrived in the roads badly damaged by a mine.

The 508 ton steam hopper *Franklin*, carrying a general cargo from Cardiff, capsized at anchor in Mumbles roads during a north-west gale accompanied by heavy seas, on the evening of 24 October 1917. The chief mate, cook, a fireman and a seaman, abandoned from one side of the vessel but were drowned, while the master and eight others put off in the boat from the other. The boat was swamped but the nine were picked up by the pilot cutter *Beaufort*. On Wednesday 5 December, the 575 ton steamship *Seaforth*, Barry to St Malo with coal, struck the submerged wreck of the *Franklin* and foundered within ten minutes. Her master and ten hands were picked up and landed at Swansea. The *Seaforth's* owners, Alfred J. Smith of Bristol, attempted to sue the Admiralty who, they claimed, had left the *Franklin's* wreck unmarked but, as it was Trinity House which was responsible, the case was thrown out. In April the following year, both wrecks were raised, beached at Mumbles, pumped out and got to Swansea for repair.

Wreckage was seen on the Mixon on the morning of 7 November 1918. A search found no sign of the crew of the vessel, the Padstow ketch *Trebiskin*.

Fog caused the 381 ton steamer *Nanset*, of Christiania, to strand in Oxwich Bay on the morning of Tuesday 26 November 1918. Her crew landed safely in their boats but the vessel capsized on the beach. Harris Bros. of Swansea Dry Dock attempted salvage but the vessel was eventually broken up for scrap.

Another vessel stranded on the morning of 2 December 1918, and made such an impression that she is still recalled by many people. The *S.S. Tours*, bound from St Nazaire to Swansea in ballast, went ashore at Deepslade Bay (popularly called Hunt's Bay) to the west of Pwll Du Head. The Loss Book at Lloyd's carries the comment "not much damaged, expect to get off". Tugs failed to refloat the vessel and she was eventually sold where she lay to C.M. Peel and Co. for just £1,200. The vessel was sold on to a salvage syndicate for £4,500 and they appointed a Mr Towers to supervise the operation. The vessel was still ashore the following spring and was visited by thousands of people each weekend. The salvage operation was followed with great interest and a new verse to a popular song was penned:

"The *Tours* is on the Gower rocks, parlez vous
The *Tours* is on the Gower rocks, parlez vous
The *Tours* is on the Gower rocks,
We don't give a damn if they don't get her off !
Inkey, pinkey, parlez vous."

The divers and support team involved in raising the *Franklin* and *Seaforth*. *(M. A. Clare, author's collection)*

The salvage vessel *Nil Desperandum* and her crew with the ship *Seaforth* which they raised in April 1918. The *Seaforth* sank on 5 December 1917 after striking the submerged wreck of the *Franklin*. *(M. A. Clare, author's collection)*

However, Towers and his gang persevered and reward came on the evening of Sunday 29 June 1919. Rocks between the vessel and the shore had been blasted away and timber skids placed under the hull. Before all was ready, the vessel slid forty or fifty feet down the skids and, as the tide rose, she floated free. The tugs *Challenger, Staghound* and *Foxhound* took her in tow to the cheers of hundreds of spectators. David Jones, who farmed Hareslade for many years, was then a boy and still remembers his disappointment at missing the event; though he had spent many hours watching the salvage team, he was at chapel that evening.

While operations continued on the *Tours*, there was yet another stranding. The 2,900 ton *S.S. Tyne*, of the Royal Mail Line, groped her way up channel on 19 April 1919. She had loaded cement at London and was bound to Swansea to complete a cargo for

Santos when, in thick mist, she collided with the brigantine *Fleur de Marie*, of St Servan, which had left Cardiff with coal. The Frenchmen were picked up by the *Tyne* just as their vessel sank. Six hours later, at a little after 9 a.m., the *Tyne* ran aground on Rother's Sker (better known as Crab Island) a little to the east of Rotherslade. The Charlton Salvage Co. of Grimsby jettisoned some of the cement (which still lies on the rocks) and the ship was refloated by the tugs *Challenger* and *Recovery* on the 29th.

Two local men watched as a sailing vessel was driven ashore on Oxwich Point on the morning of 9 July 1920. Seeing a man on board, they scrambled over the rocks to assist but, as the man prepared to jump overboard, the vessel's mast fell killing him. A National Insurance card in the name of Augustine O'Shea, and fourteen £1 notes washed in. O'Shea

The Norwegian ship *Nanset* stranded on Oxwich beach in fog on 26 November 1918. The crew got ashore but the vessel capsized and was scrapped. *(W. T. Goldsworthy collection)*

The *Tours*, St Nazaire to Swansea in ballast, went ashore in Hunt's Bay on 2 December 1918. It took seven months to refloat her. *(M. A. Clare, Ken Reeves collection)*

The *Tours* ready for refloating. *(M. A. Clare, Ken Reeves collection)*

The salvage gang whose months of hard work resulted in the refloating of the *Tours*. (M. A. Clare, author's collection)

had bought the vessel, the former Cardiff pilot skiff *Primrose*, in order to return to Ireland. His body was recovered that evening and lies buried in Oxwich churchyard.

The Breton schooner *Raven*, sailed from Swansea on 19 October 1923 with coal for St Brieuc. She was found to be leaking and put back for Mumbles where she was re-caulked. On the 27th she sailed for Swansea for further repairs but ran aground at the harbour entrance. Her signals of distress brought the lifeboat *Charlie Medland* across the bay on her last service. The crew of five were saved just as the schooner's deck began to break up.

Soon after 5 o'clock on the morning of Tuesday 8 January 1924 John Webber, a retired Swansea jeweller living at Pennard, was roused by distress rockets. He and his son lit hurricane lamps and walked to the cliff above Heatherslade. They discovered the steamship *Fellside* hard ashore and had a brief shouted conversation with the crew. Mr Webber sent his son to Oxwich on foot to inform the coastguard. Meanwhile the crew abandoned in two boats. Twelve crew got ashore in one but the other boat capsized drowning a seaman. The Belfast registered vessel, which was bound to Swansea with pitwood, became a total loss and was scrapped by Greening & Co. of Killay.

The Kinsale owned schooner *Harry Herbert* was bound to Liverpool with a cargo of timber when she was disabled by a gale and driven up channel. She stranded and was wrecked on the Lynch on Wednesday 3 March 1926. Her crew got ashore and the remains of the vessel were washed up at Burry Holms.

On the afternoon of 15 November 1926 the harbourmaster at Swansea was alerted by Lands End Radio and asked to prepare for the arrival of the

The *S.S. Tyne* stranded on Rother's Sker on 19 April 1919 after being in collision in fog with a brigantine. *(M. A. Clare, author's collection).*

steamship *Cranstone* which had a fire in her cargo of lignite. On passage from Hamburg to Liverpool with the cargo, which was badly needed in Britain due to the general strike, the crew of the 1,740 ton vessel had discovered the fire when passing the Isle of Wight. They fought a losing battle with the flames and, on rounding Lands End, the master, Capt Thompson, had decided to run for Swansea. The ship arrived off Mumbles late that evening her sides red hot and twenty foot flames rising from the fore-

hold. The tugs *Trusty, Herculaneum* and *Mumbles* beached the ship and got their hoses into action, but the fire was finally extinguished only when the vessel was scuttled in the shallows. After the ship had cooled, the remains of the cargo were discharged and she was refloated.

The ketch *Gloria*, owned by Mrs Scott landlady of the Victoria Inn, Mumbles, was fishing in Carmarthen Bay when a gale blew up on Tuesday 6 December 1927. The master, Robert Reynolds,

The *Tyne* uses her derricks to discharge some of her cargo of cement. The vessel was refloated after ten days. (*M. A. Clare, author's collection*).

The schooner *Fleur de France* stranded on the Mixon on 2 April 1920. She is seen here beached off the promenade at Mumbles awaiting repair. *(W. T. Goldsworthy collection)*

sought shelter at Rhosili but the vessel was swamped and sank at her anchors. Reynolds and his crew abandoned in the boat and were helped ashore by a party of auxiliary coastguards.

The Swansea trawlers *Carew Castle*, *Clyne Castle* and *Radnor Castle* were returning from a fishing trip on the evening of Thursday 31 October 1929 when the first vessel entered a fog bank and ran aground near Culver Hole on the west side of Port Eynon Point. The vessel was holed and the engine room flooded. Whittaker, the radio operator, raised the alarm via Fishguard Radio and was then able to contact the *Radnor Castle* which stood by. The falling tide allowed skipper Joe Boyce and his crew of ten to walk ashore. The trawler became a total loss.

The *S.S. Fellside* ashore at Heatherslade, Pennard, on 8 January 1924. The vessel, bound to Swansea with pitwood, became a total loss. *(M. A. Clare, author's collection)*

The 195 ton tug *Mumbles*, owned by the British Tanker Co., was returning up channel, having assisted the disabled tanker *British Motorist*, when she ran ashore in thick fog and driving rain to the west of Oxwich Point on the morning of 25 February 1931. The crew abandoned and were given shelter by Lady Blythswood of Penrice. The Swansea tug *Herculaneum* failed to refloat the vessel and she broke up.

Soon after midnight on 18 December 1933 the 255 ton *S.S. Ben Blanche*, of Ramsey, Isle of Man, struck the rocks below Paviland Cliffs in very thick weather. Mumbles lifeboat *Edward, Prince of Wales* launched at 2.15 a.m. and reached the spot at 5.15 to find the ship submerged. Searching off shore, the lifeboat found the crew of seven in their boats and picked them up. The vessel, bound from Dundrum to Swansea with 150 tons of potatoes for Fred Ley & Sons, became a total loss.

On the evening of Sunday 10 January 1937, Burnham Radio picked up a message from the trawler *Roche Castle* reporting that she was ashore "about ten miles west of Mumbles". The coastguard was informed, Mumbles lifeboat launched, and search parties organised along the coast. The trawler, belonging to Consolidated Fisheries and returning to Swansea with its catch, was found at the foot of Paviland Cliffs. The lifeboat and trawlers *Powis Castle* and *Grosmont Castle* stood by but the vessel was too close in for them to get near. Rhosili L.S.A. company, led by Station Officer S.T. Owen, got a line aboard and the breeches buoy rigged, but

The *Cranstone*, of Newcastle, was scuttled off Mumbles to put out a fire in her cargo of lignite which she was carrying from Hamburg to Liverpool during the general strike of 1926. *(W. T. Goldsworthy collection)*

The tug *Mumbles* stranded on Oxwich Point in fog on 25 February 1931 and became a total loss. *(W. T. Goldsworthy collection)*

the master hoped to refloat the trawler on the flood. When the tide rose, the vessel began to heel towards the shore and was swept by heavy seas. The crew were now anxious to abandon and two men got into the buoy. As it was being hauled ashore, the hawser went slack as the vessel worked and then jerked taut throwing one of the men, George Gaylor of Swansea, into the sea where he was drowned. In less than an hour the master James Insole; the mate, his brother Ivor; and the remaining eight members of the crew were rescued. The District Officer of the coastguard, A.J. Jeffers, and a member of the rocket crew went down onto the rocks to assist the survivors ashore and to prevent the lines getting foul of the rocks. Also in attendance was the coastguard inspector, Commander R.G. Hurst R.N., and his report of the rescue led to the Rhosili company being awarded the Board of Trade Wreck Shield. Officer Jeffers was presented with a silver salver.

A very heavy gale struck on Saturday 15 January 1938 causing a great deal of damage along the coast of Wales. The next day, two bodies were found on Rhosili beach and a ship's boats came ashore at Port Eynon and Oxwich. They were found to belong to the Swansea registered *Glanrhyd*, 1,525 tons gross, owned by Harries Bros. of Gloucester Place. The ship had left Newport at 2.30 p.m. on Friday with coal duff for Manchester. Owen L. Harries of the owners went to Llangennith where he identified one of the bodies as that of the vessel's master, Capt Norman Seawert. Over the next few days a further six bodies were recovered along the coast between Slade and Whitford. The Wreck Commissioner held an inquiry into the *Glanrhyd's* loss and concluded that the vessel and her crew of seventeen had probably been overwhelmed by exceptionally large seas and had foundered off shore possibly in the vicinity of the Helwick lightship.

The trawler *Roche Castle* was wrecked at Paviland on 10 January 1937. The Rhosili L.S.A. company saved all but one of the eleven man crew. *(Gerald Holman, Gareth Mills collection)*

WAR AGAIN

During the second World War a number of ships were mined, and damaged or sunk in the approaches to Swansea. In the first week of October 1939 the *Lochgoil* and *Marwarri* were both damaged by mines and beached at Mumbles for repair. The first major casualty was the Alfred Holt ship *Protesilaus*, 9,577 tons gross, in ballast from Liverpool to Barry, which was mined about six miles W.S.W. of Mumbles Head on 21 January 1940. Twenty of her crew of sixty were injured by the explosion of a magazine. The vessel was then beached on the mud flats off Oystermouth but broke in two. Months later, the fore part was towed to Briton Ferry and then to Scotland for use as a block-ship at Scapa Flow, but developed a serious leak en route and was sunk by gunfire.

Mumbles lifeboat was launched at 2.15 on the morning of 7 February 1940 to the assistance of a steamship aground at Port Eynon. She was the 5,184 ton *Eldonpark*, of Glasgow, Bona (Algeria) to Port Talbot with much needed iron ore. It has always been assumed that this ship too had been mined but it appears that this was not the case. Lloyd's casualty book states that she stranded on the Helwick in thick weather, accompanied by a heavy ground sea, was badly damaged and beached at Port Eynon in a sinking condition. The ship was virtually submerged but, after a skilful and daring rescue, Coxswain William Davies and his men succeeded in saving the master and crew of thirty six. The vessel was allowed to break up, but being a

hazard to navigation the wreckage was dispersed after the war.

In recent years sub-aqua enthusiasts have become excited by the rumour that a German U-boat was sunk about four miles off Oxwich Point in the spring of 1940. The story began with the memoirs of Donald Chapman who was a coastguard auxiliary at Oxwich during the war. However, papers supplied by the Ministry of Defence show that the incident, on 25 March 1940, occurred at a bearing of 327 degrees 0.5 miles off Bull Point, North Devon, which is about 15 miles S.W. by S. of Oxwich Point. Furthermore, though H.M. trawlers *Kirkella* and *Bandolero* depth charged a target, and opened fire on it when it came to the surface, the Admiralty U-boat Assessment Committee concluded that it was a "non-submarine" (presumably an existing wreck), and this seems to have been confirmed after the war when documents seized from the Kriegsmarine established that no U-boats were operating in the Bristol Channel at the time. Whatever the truth of the matter, George Lilley skipper of the *Kirkella*, received the D.S.C. in July 1940.

A wreck off Mumbles which is still a popular fishing mark is that of the 6,549 ton whale-factory ship *Strombus*, of Tonsberg (Norway). The vessel, bound from Swansea to the Antarctic with coal and patent fuel, struck a mine on 26 October 1940 about two miles east of Mumbles Head. All forty members of the crew survived, but the ship broke

The *Protesilaus* bound from Liverpool to Barry in ballast, has broken in two after being mined six miles WSW of Mumbles Head on 21 January 1940. *(W. T. Goldsworthy collection)*

Bound from Bona to Port Talbot with iron ore, the *Eldonpark* stranded on the Helwick in thick weather and was beached at Port Eynon on 7 February 1940. *(W. T. Goldsworthy collection)*

in two. The after part capsized and sank, but the fore section was beached and, two years later, towed to Briton Ferry for breaking.

At 9 a.m. on 12 November 1940 Mumbles lifeboat was returning from an unsuccessful call to a casualty ashore at Ogmore, east of Porthcawl. A westerly storm of near hurricane force was blowing. Mumbles coastguard signalled the boat to proceed .

to another casualty at Overton. Having battled against the storm for a further hour, the lifeboat was recalled when it was learnt that the crew had got ashore safely. The casualty was the Rotterdam registered salvage tug *Wittezee*, Falmouth to Lamlash (Firth of Clyde) on naval service. When the vessel drove ashore in Overton Mere, police constable Mabbett and a group of coastguards led by station officer Dodd, were quickly on the scene. Dodd rescued the tug's master from the surf, and then persuaded the rest of the crew to remain aboard until the ebb. For their gallantry each member of the rescue party was decorated by the Netherlands government. The tug became a complete wreck and was broken up for scrap. Her skipper presented the tug's wheel to the landlord of the Ship Inn at Port Eynon who fed and clothed them after rescue.

The 5,261 ton *Fort Medine*, Wabana (Newfoundland) to Port Talbot with a cargo of 7,000 tons of iron ore, fell victim to a mine on 20 February 1941. The ship sank rapidly a mile or so east of Mumbles Head, but the forty six survivors were picked up by the pilot cutter. Eight days later the 534 ton motor vessel *Cabenda*, of London, Shoreham to Briton Ferry with 600 tons of scrap, was also mined and sank rapidly east of Mumbles Head, drowning a member of the crew.

The ship *London II*, Manchester to Cardiff with

The World War II destroyer *Cleveland* straddles the stream known as Diles Lake on Rhosili beach. The vessel was on her way to be broken up when she parted her tow on 28 June 1957. *(World Ship Society Photo Library)*

steel billets and scrap, was bombed by enemy air-craft a few miles south-west of the Helwick light-ship on 21 March 1941. Four of the eighteen crew were killed and the vessel was abandoned on fire. She drifted up the coast and sank six miles south-west of Mumbles Head. On the same day the 617 ton *Millisle*, Cardiff to Cork with coal, was bombed and sunk two miles east of the lightship drowning nine of the crew and the gunner.

Many people recall the section of a tanker which lay close inshore at Oxwich for many years, the remains of which may still be seen at low water. She was the 8,262 ton Norwegian motor vessel *Solor*, carrying fuel oil and a deck-cargo of crated gliders from New York for the Clyde. On 27 January 1945 she was torpedoed in the Irish Sea with the loss of four of her crew of forty four. The ship was beached at Oxwich two days later to allow her cargo to be discharged. When the hull broke in two, the aft section was towed to Briton Ferry for breaking.

A bulldozer is used to move sand in preparation for an attempt at refloating the Cleveland. *(World Ship Society Photo Library)*

Attempting to refloat the *Cleveland* on an evening tide. When all attempts failed the destroyer was scrapped on the beach. *(Photo taken by Mike Davies of Cadoxton, Neath)*

The fore section remained at Oxwich until broken up for scrap.

The *S.S. Riverton*, 7,345 tons gross, was torpedoed in a position about fifteen miles north of St Ives on 23 April 1945. The badly damaged stern section was removed when the ship was beached between Mumbles lighthouse and the pier. The ship had a new stern fitted and resumed trading after the war.

*   *   *   *   *   *

The years since the war have seen few shipwrecks and the Gower coast has become a centre for watersports - angling, sailing, diving, surfing and boating in general. The coastguard and lifeboat crews now have a different, but no less onerous, task. Those few incidents which have occurred have hit the headlines if only for a few days. Perhaps the wreck which had the greatest impact without adversely affecting anyone was that of the destroyer *Cleveland*. At 6.30 on the evening of Friday 28 June 1957 she parted from the tug *Brynforth*, which was towing her from Cardiff to the breakers at Llanelli, and ran well up onto the beach at Diles Lake,

Over four hundred passengers were rescued from the *Prince Ivanhoe* which became a wreck after striking rocks off Port Eynon Point on 3 August 1981. (*Advert 'Herald of Wales'*)

The *Prince Ivanhoe* lies stranded at Port Eynon. She was abandoned by the underwriters and broke up in the winter gales. *(Author's photo)*

Llangennith. Countless attempts failed to refloat the vessel on the highest tides and her owners, the British Iron and Steel Corporation, were forced to scrap her where she lay.

The 986 ton motor vessel *Prince Ivanhoe*, owned by the Firth of Clyde Steam Packet Co. and operated by Waverley Excursions Ltd, began cruising the Bristol Channel on the old paddle steamer routes in 1981. On Monday 3 August that year the vessel called at Penarth, Barry and Minehead before arriv-

ing at Mumbles Pier to begin a Gower cruise. Over four hundred passengers crowded the decks, bar and buffet of the well-appointed ship as she made her way along the coast on a fine summer afternoon, but shortly after 3.30 the rescue services were alerted when the coastguard at Mumbles received a distress message from her. The *Prince Ivanhoe* had been sailing close inshore and had struck on the submerged reef off Port Eynon Point. The vessel was immediately put about and run

The wrecked remains of the *Prince Ivanhoe* . *(Gareth Mills collection)*

ashore at Horton just yards from the beach and the inshore lifeboat station. Lifeboats, search and rescue helicopters, and numerous pleasure craft took part in the rescue of passengers and crew, and all were got safely ashore. Sadly two passengers collapsed with heart attacks and one died.

The wreck of the *Prince Ivanhoe* was abandoned by the underwriters and broke up in the winter gales. Her wreckage, however, proved to be a serious hazard to small boats and particularly to the Horton inshore lifeboat. At length, a Falmouth salvage company undertook the removal of the wreck on behalf of Trinity House. A south-westerly gale on 2 September 1983 drove the salvage vessels *Tom Jay* and *Seawork Samson*, which were carrying out the work, from their moorings and onto the beach between Horton and Slade. When the weather moderated, the vessels were refloated and finished the task of removing Gower's most recent substantial wreck.

Meanwhile the yacht *Jolani* had been wrecked on Oxwich beach late on the evening of Thursday 8 October 1981. The Dugdale family, from Cheshire, had built the 43 ft yacht themselves and intended making a world cruise. They had been sheltering at Oxwich for some days, when the anchor cables parted and the yacht was driven by storm force winds onto the beach. The rescue services were alerted and Mumbles lifeboat launched but a quick turn-out by the coastguard rescue company at Oxwich saved Eric Dugdale, his wife Jenny, and children Laura, Jon and Nichola. The Oxwich company were presented with the Rescue Shield by Iain Sproat, Under Secretary of State for Trade, at a ceremony attended by Eric Dugdale who said "We shall owe a debt of gratitude to these men for the rest of our lives. What do you say when you have

been handed back your lives by such men as these? We are all of us very, very grateful to them". It was the second occasion that the shield had come to Gower since it was instituted in 1923, for it was the same award (then known as the Wreck Shield) won by the Rhosili L.S.A. for the *Roche Castle* service in 1937.

Though shipwrecks on the peninsula are thankfully now rare, it is too much to think that they are completely a thing of the past, or that the people of Gower will no longer see shattered hulls, or shocked and bedraggled survivors, or have the sad task of recovering and burying the dead. When incidents do occur however, the rescue services, with the versatility of modern lifeboats and helicopters and the skill, initiative and courage of their crews, will be ever ready to respond.

The salvage vessels *Seawork Samson* and *Tom Jay* were driven ashore at Horton in September 1983. Engaged in clearing the wreck of the *Prince Ivanhoe*, their cables parted in a gale. *(Author's photo)*

INDEX

Lifeboats:

A Daughter's Offering (Port Eynon) 57
Charlie Medland (Mumbles) 85
City of Bath (Pembrey) 41
Edward, Prince of Wales (Mumbles) 90
Harbour Trust (Swansea) 23
James & Elizabeth (Llanelli) 44
Janet (Port Eynon) 71, 75
Martha & Anne (Mumbles) 41
Rescue (Llanelli) 35
Stanton Meyrick of Pimlico (Pembrey) 46
Wolverhampton (Mumbles) 53

Shipwrecks:

A

Admiral Prinz Adalbert 53
Agnes 57
Agnes Jack 53
Alarm 50
Albion 42
Althea 61
Amethyst 25, 43
Anemone 42
Angally 21
Ann 43
Anna Catherine 35
Anne 31
Ann & Elizabeth 30

Ann & Sarah 19
Antonio Luca 47
Appledram 20
Argus 57
Arietta 33
Artistic 44
Atlas 21

B

Benamain 61
Ben Blanche 90
Bluebell 74
Bonny Kate 21
Bougainville 68
Bounty Hall 20
Brechin Castle 32
Brigand 45
Bristol Packet 67
Britannia 19, 26, 49
Brothers 18, 19, 43
Busy 37

C

Cabenda 96
Caesar 13
Camille 38
Carew Castle 88
Caroline Phillips 49
Catherine Jenkins 36
Charioteer 72
Charles 30
Charlotte 14
Charming Nancy 12
Chasseur 41

Chebucto 46
Circassian 32
City of Bristol 28
Cleveland 99
Corliana 44
Cornish Diamond 45
Corundum 75
Courageux 34
Cranstone 87
Cresswell 51

D

Daring 45
Dart 30
Desirée 40
Dextrous 49
Diligence 20, 26
Dolphin 27
Duisberg 66

E

Eagle 13, 33
Earl Gowrie 33
Eldonpark 93
Electric Flash 41
Eliza 15, 38, 44
Elizabeth 19, 48
Elizabeth Jane 75
Eliza Jane 27, 41
Ellen 35
Emily 37
Emmanuel Adrien 41
Emmet 37
Endeavour 14

Epidauro 74
Espérance 72
Espoir 41

F

Fanny 17, 29
Favourite 25, 61
Felicité 61
Fellside 86
Feronia 27
Fort Medine 96
Fortuna 42
France 50
Frances 31
Frances Anne 25
Francis & Ann 40
Franklin 79
Friends 21, 38
Friendship 13, 19

G

George 20, 22
Geraldine 52
Glanrhyd 92
Gleaning 49
Glenravil Miner 63
Gloria 87
Grace 27
Gurnet 30

H

Happy Return 37, 51
Harry Herbert 86
Haswell 50
Hayle Trader 15
Hazard 37, 46
Hectorine 40
Helvetia 57
Henry 23

Henry Edmunds 60
Hero 21, 26
H.L.C. 61
Hope 17, 34, 47
Huntress 43

I

Idas 23
Ierne 67
Ilfracombe Packet 23
Imbros 65
Indefatigable 67
Industrious 40
Industry 30
Irish Miners 23
Irma 35

J

Jane 22, 60, 69
Jenny 49
Jeremiah 27
Jeune Celine 43
J.K. Allport 67
J.O. 39
John 20
Jolani 102
Joseph et Marie 45
Juanita 37
Julia 31
Juno 22
J.W.J. 55

L

Laconic 39
Lady of the Lake 40
La Manche 20
Lammershagen 52
Lavinia 21
Leonora 74

Leverpool 15
Lively 22
Liverpool Packet 30
Lochgoil 93
London II 96
Lord Marmion 54
Lord Nelson 19
Louis 37
Lovely Betsey 15

M

Margaret 25, 31
Margaret Ann 47
Maria 65
Marie Therese 68
Marwarri 93
Mary 25, 31, 34, 45
Mary Ann 26
Mary Fanny 43
Mary Jones 34
Menai 21
Mercia 75
Mercur 50
Milan 59
Millisle 97
Monkey 37
Mumbles 90

N

Nancy 19
Nanset 79
Neptune 15, 37
Nettuno 35
New Blessing 26
Nieuwe Goude Spoor 12
Notre Dame de Lourdes 69
Novo Moro 17
Nuavo Plauto 44

O

Odysseus 47
Olga 75
Onward 43

P

Paladino 47
Parry's Lodge 53
Pascoe Grenfell 37
Peri 40
Petersburg 26
Pioneer 37
Ponsonby 21
Pretty Maggy 35
Primrose 85
Prince Ivanhoe 100
Priscilla 15
Prophete Elie 57
Protesilaus 93

R

Raven 85
Rebecca 30
Recovery 17
Reine des Fleurs 54
René 55
Resolution 15
Reverie 50
Riverton 99
Robert Henry 38
Robert Williams 53
Robin Hood 41
Roche Castle 90
Roscius 43
Rose 17

S

Saetia Mazzed 14
Saint Louis 79

St Christophe 79
Sally & William 20
Samuel 55
Sarah 38
Sarah & Rachel 30
Sarah Jane 35
Sarsfield 61
Seaflower 14, 22
Seaforth 79
Shepherd 27
Shepton Mallet 12
Sicie 72
Sisters 15, 27
Smiling Morn 65
Sofia 50
Solor 97
Speculator 22
Spreacombe 30
Spring Flower 34
Strombus 93
Suir 27
Superior 30
Surprise 25, 54
Swiftsure 37
Syren 25

T

Thames 57
Thetis 31
Three Brothers 21
Three Sisters 65
Tidy 51
Tilly 67
Tivyside 67
Tours 79
Trafalgar 20
Trebiskin 79
Tridonia 75
Triton 31, 48

Two Sisters 13, 17
Tyne 81

U

U-boat 93
Union 21, 38
Unity 17

V

Vauban 55
Vennerne 63
Vesta 41
Victoria 33
Victoria & Albert 39
Villiers 38

W

Wasp 64
Water Lily 43
Wave 37
Western Star 37
William & Mary 22, 38
Wiln 69
Wittezee 95

X

Xanthippe 55

Z

Zenith 41
Zoe 38, 65